California State & Local Government In Crisis
Copyright 1992, 1995, 1997, 2000, 2004, 2006, 2018 - 7th Edition

Educational Textbook Company
P.O. Box 3597
Covina, California 91722
(626) 339-7733
FAX (626) 332-4744
www.etctextbooks.com

Includes Index.

Library of Congress Cataloging in Publication Data

Huber, Walter Roy
California State & Local Government in Crisis

ISBN 978-16-2684-014-0

320.9794

1. California Politics and Government
2. Political Participation

I. Huber, Walter R., 1941 II. Title.

Printed in Marina del Rey, California, U.S.A.

Thanks to Our Production Team!

Colleen Taber: Executive Editor
Rick Lee: Layout and Pre-Press Editor
Shelley Geary: PowerPoint®, Canvas®
Philip Dockter: Art Director
Melinda Winters: Cover Art Design
Troy Monroe Stacey: Cover Design

Preface

The last general election was an unprecedented "BOMB SHELL" for many reasons. It was the most polarizing and controversial presidential election in our lifetime. Trump's surprising election as president can't be ignored by a premium California textbook, as national, state, and local politics are already intersecting on many levels. This is not a book for the faint of heart  or students who don't want to have their world disrupted by addressing difficult and touchy subjects. Change is already in the wind.

We address state issues like the passing of Prop 64 legalizing recreational marijuana (both positive and negative), as well as the pressing issue of immigration—a subject close to many of our students' hearts.

We give you the facts and let you choose how you want to interpret them. You need to anticipate how Donald Trump's policies and an all Republican federal government may affect this state. As California is a Democratic Supermajority (Governor, State Assembly and Senate, and State Supreme Court) there is bound to be trouble in paradise.

"Students beware! Between the conservative Trump administration and California's liberal attitude, you can expect very contentious politics for the next four years." –Walt Huber

We break down California politics from its basic nuts and bolts all the way up to the more complicated issues facing us today— financial, environmental, and social.

 This book doesn't tell you what to think, but it does tell you what happened in the past and in the present to allow you to form your own opinions. Whether you see the future as being on the precipice of disaster or on the verge of becoming "great again" this book will give you the tools to understand how the national forum affects us all on a state and local level.

The time for complacency is over. We all have a horse in this race.

On one hand: Mr. Trump has openly called global warming a hoax, whereas Californians are notorious environmentalists—a potential  butting of heads when national policy conflicts with state concerns. With two of the largest ports in the country located in California, Trump's trade policies will have a direct effect on the shipping and import/export industry that feeds those ports. Most important of all, however, may be the appointment of conservative, pro-life Supreme Court judges who sit on the bench for life. When important court cases in California work their way up the judicial ladder until they reach the highest court in the land, new ears will be hearing those cases, and no doubt rule very differently than a liberal court. Women fear for their reproductive rights, immigrants fear deportation, farmers fear for a lack of itinerant farm labor, minorities fear for their civil rights… basically Californians are by and large fearful of this new regime.

On the other hand: Many voters believed that a new type of President was needed—one who promised jobs and prosperity, when they felt left behind. Trump's slogan "Let's Make America Great Again" apparently motivated enough Americans to come out and vote for him. His history of being a successful businessman was what many believed gave him a new perspective on the Presidency with a focus on business and less big government–leaving it up to the states to decide important issues on their own (a sentiment shared by the founding fathers.)

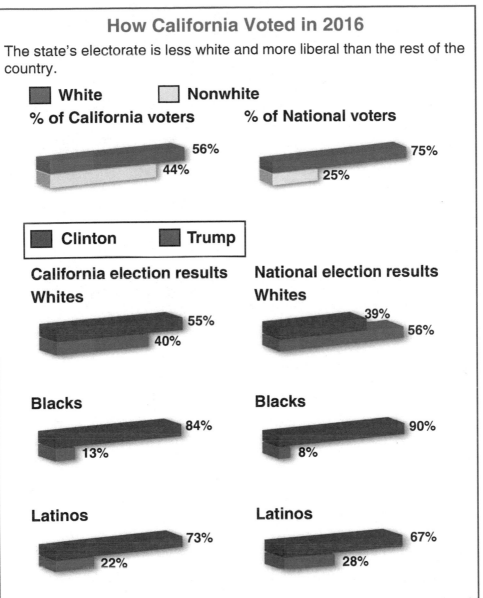

How California Voted in 2016

The state's electorate is less white and more liberal than the rest of the country.

■ White   □ Nonwhite

% of California voters

56%
44%

% of National voters

75%
25%

■ Clinton   ■ Trump

California election results
Whites

55%
40%

National election results
Whites

39%
56%

Blacks

84%
13%

Blacks

90%
8%

Latinos

73%
22%

Latinos

67%
28%

Sources: USC Dornsife/L.A. Times postelection poll, SurveyMonkey national postelection poll.

Acknowledgements

We acknowledge the following instructors for their hard work in teaching political science (no endorsement implied).

American River College
  Tamir Sukkary
  Tressa Tabares
  Kathleen Collihan
  Jason Vitiach

Antelope Valley College
  Donald R. Ranish

Bakersfield College
  Steven Holmes

Chaffee College
  Kevin Cameron

Citrus College
  Gerhard Peters

College of San Mateo
  Leighton D. Armitage
  Dan Kaplan

College of San Mateo
  Lee R. Miller, Ph.D.

Cosumnes River College
  M. Morales
  Winsome Jackson
  Elizabeth Huffman

Cypress College
  Guinevere Hodges

East Los Angeles College
  Kenneth Chairprasert

Long Beach City College
  Paul Savoie

Long Beach City College
  Laura Pellegrini

Los Angeles City College
  Joseph Meyer

Los Angeles City College
  Ronald Pelton

Los Angeles Trade Tech College
  Lionel B. Coulter, Ph.D

Los Angeles Trade Tech College
  Akop Baltayan, CPA, Esquire

Mission College
  Kathryn Wood

Mt. San Antonio College
  Kelly Rivera

Mt. San Antonio College
  James Stone

Palomar College
  Joseph Limer

Palo Verde College
  Kevin Eoff, Sr.

Pasadena City College
  David S. McCabe

Pierce College
  Anthony Gabrielli
  Denise Munro Robb, Ph.D.

Sacramento City College
  Syreeta Harada

Saddleback College
  Glenna Piera

San Bernardino Valley College
  Riase Jakpor, Ph.D.

San Diego City College
  Myles L. Clowers
  Donald H. Estes

San Diego Mesa College
  J. Avorh

San Joaquin Delta College
  Cirian Villavencio

Skyline College
  Johannes Masare

Ventura College
  Dr. Farzeen Nasri

West Los Angeles College
  Jack D. Ruebensaal

West Valley College
  Nicola Guitierrez

Occidental College
  Peter Dreiser

University of San Diego
  Kimberly Fletcher, Ph.D.
  Ronnee Schreiber, Ph.D.

Table of Contents

California Facts

State Capitals of California

San Jose: November 13, 1849 to May 1, 1851

Vallejo: January 5, 1852 to February 4, 1853

(Temporarily in Sacramento January 16, 1852 to May 4, 1852)

Benicia: February 4, 1853 to February 25, 1854

Sacramento: February 25, 1854 to Present

San Francisco: January 24, 1862 to May 15, 1862 (Temporary)

Sacramento: 1869 Permanent Quarters

State Motto: "Eureka" (I have found it)

State Bird: California Quail (Lophortyx californica)

State Flower: California Golden Poppy (Eschsholtzia californica)

State Tree: California Redwood - The Coast Redwood (Sequoia sempervirens) and the Giant Sequoia (Sequoia gigantea)

State Reptile: The Desert Tortoise (Gopherus agassizi)

State Animal: The California Grizzly Bear (Ursus californicus)

State Folk Dance: Square Dance

State Marine Fish: The Garibaldi (Hypsypops rubicundus)

State Colors: Blue and Gold

State Marine Animal: The California Gray Whale (Eschrichtius robustus)

State Insect: The California Dogface Butterfly (Zerene eurydice)

State Mineral: Gold

State Rock: Serpentine

State Soil: The San Joaquin Soil

State Gemstone: Benitoite

State Prehistoric Artifact: The Chipped Stone Bear

State Fossil: The Sabre-Tooth Cat (Smilodon californicus)

State Fish: The Golden Trout (Salmo agua-bonita)

State Dance: West Coast Swing Dancing

State Theater: Pasadena Playhouse

State Fife & Drum Band: The California Consolidated Drum Band

State Song: "I Love You, California", written by F.B. Silverwood

Size: The third largest state, 163,707 square miles

Statehood: The 31st State. Admitted Sept. 9, 1850

Highest Point: Mt. Whitney at 14,494 feet above sea level

Lowest Point: Death Valley at 282 feet below sea level

Geographic Center of the State: 38 miles east of Madera

California's 1st Suspension Bridge: Built in 1856, was relocated in Bidwell Canyon prior to the construction of the Oroville Dam.

Number of Counties: 58

Alpine, Mariposa, and Trinity Counties: No incorporated cities within their borders.

Incorporated Cities in California: 477

Number of Chartered Cities: 105

Number of General Law Cities: 372

Total Land Area: 155,973 square miles

Total Water Area: 7,734 square miles

Shoreline: 3,427 miles

Coastline: 840 miles

Did You Know...

Spanish navigator Juan Rodríguez Cabrillo became the first European in recorded history to sight the region that is present-day California in 1542.

California is the most populous state (and the third largest by area). To put California's population, approximately 38 million people, in perspective, one out of every eight Americans is from California.

Fortune cookie, Apple computer, theme park (Disneyland), Frisbee, blue jeans and the Barbie doll are all invented in California.

San Francisco Bay is the world's largest landlocked harbor.

California's Mount Whitney measures as the highest peak in the lower 48 states. Its most famous climb is Mount Whitney Trail to the 14,495 feet summit.

More turkeys are raised in California than in any other state in the United States.

Castroville is known as the Artichoke Capital of the World. In 1947, a young woman named Norma Jean was crowned Castroville's first Artichoke Queen. She later became world-famous actress by her screen name, Marilyn Monroe.

The original California flag, the first Bear Flag, was designed by William L. Todd, Abraham Lincoln's relative by marriage (William L. Todd was a cousin of Abraham Lincoln's wife, Mary Todd Lincoln).

California is the first state ever to become a trillion dollar economy in gross state product. If California were a country, it would be the sixth largest economy in the world.

San Francisco population grew 180 times during the seven years of Goldrush (1848 - 1855), from about 200 to over 36,000.

California produces about 60% of peaches harvested in USA. Palmetto State (South Carolina) is distant second with about 15%. Peach State (Georgia) produces about 13% of Peaches harvested in USA!

California is the largest grape producing state in the United States. California is also the largest wine producing state in the USA.

California accounts for about half of fruit acreage in USA.

California is the largest producer of almonds in the world. The Golden State produces over 80% of the global production of almonds!

*Professor Hubie® points
to interesting websites.*

Chapter 1

California in Crisis!

I. California's Newest Crisis:
President Trump's Impact on California

A. PRESIDENT TRUMP WON THE NATION, BUT NOT CALIFORNIA

President Trump's Administration, for good or bad, will now impact Californians.

For years there has been a "political utopia" in California—with a Democratic governor, legislature, state supreme court, and Obama as President.

The political reality is that the Democrats won the popular vote in California with a huge 4.2 million voter lead and all the 55 electoral college votes.

Hillary Clinton (DEM), 8,753,788. (62.2%)
Donald J. Trump (REP), 4,483,810. (31.8%)

B. DEMOCRATS—A SUPERMAJORITY IN THE STATE LEGISLATURE

California has a supermajority (two-thirds) in the state legislature. This means the Democrat-controlled state legislature (Assembly and Senate) can pass certain legislation with a two-thirds vote, regardless of how the Republicans vote.

Chapter Outline

California's high-tech digital corporations, with their highly educated employees, are making lots of money. Meanwhile, middle-income workers who, in the past, prospered in manufacturing have been pushed out because of increasing regulations. Finally, those with lower incomes and fewer skills find it hard to survive (shamefully, 20.6% live below the poverty line).

C. THE CALIFORNIA ECONOMIC CRISIS CONTINUES!

In the last decade, we have gone from a growth state to a slow-growth state.

California, the golden state, which grew for so many decades, is in the middle of the state's biggest economic change ever! Lower income individuals are leaving the state because there are fewer low-skilled jobs, while higher income individuals (i.e., tech and biotech) are arriving. Our highways are congested, schools are underfunded, housing costs are high, health care and welfare for our growing poor population is grossly inadequate, and the quality of our air and water is getting better but costing us more.

The sad fact is that there are no simple answers anymore. We keep increasing our already high state taxes (**2017—a 42% increase in gas tax from 28 cents to 40 cents a gallon**) which may pressure even more of the very people who pay the most taxes to leave the state.

II. California's Economy is Growing Again

A. CALIFORNIA IS A WORLD-CLASS ECONOMY

California is a world class economic power because it is economically diverse. *ECONOMIC DIVERSITY means that many economic activities are balanced so that no one industry dominates to the extent that, if eliminated, it would cause severe problems.* Economic power is measured by gross domestic product. *GROSS DOMESTIC PRODUCT (GDP) is the sum of all products and services produced by a country in a given year.*

California handles 21.5% of all U.S. trade (and has 12.5% of the U.S. population). We import more than we export.

Trade is clearly one of the driving industries in California. Between exports and imports, California has boosted jobs in air transportation, wholesale trades, and port facilities. Our state is outperforming the nation in exports because: 1) our major trading partners have above average economic growth and 2) our exports are concentrated in high-growth industries.

EXPORTS are manufactured goods, agricultural produce, minerals, and other items produced in the United States but purchased by other countries. Our top five export partners are: Mexico, Canada, China, Japan, and Hong Kong. *IMPORTS are goods and services purchased from other countries.* Our top four import partners are: China, Mexico, Japan, and Canada.

California's Top 5 Export Markets
(Millions of U.S. Dollars)

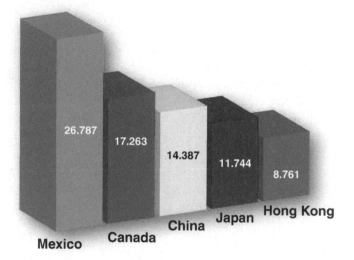

26.787 Mexico
17.263 Canada
14.387 China
11.744 Japan
8.761 Hong Kong

California's Top 5 Export Categories
(Millions of U.S. Dollars)

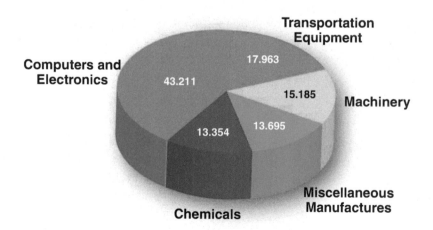

Computers and Electronics 43.211
Transportation Equipment 17.963
Machinery 15.185
Miscellaneous Manufactures 13.695
Chemicals 13.354

Source: International Trade Administration
www.trade.gov/mas/ian/statereports/states/ca.pdf

B. PRESIDENT TRUMP: INCREASE EXPORTS, REDUCE IMPORTS?

Will President Trump's trade policies be a blessing or curse? Will Trump create a new bilateral trade deal (country-to-country)?

President Trump's goal is to bring more jobs back to America by negotiating better trade deals with our major trading partners, especially Mexico. Most countries could reduce or eliminate tariffs, import quotas, export restrictions, and other trade barriers by agreeing to bilateral trade agreements.

President Trump would like to decrease imports from Mexico, our biggest trading partner. If he can't convince Mexico to reduce taxing our products and services going to Mexico, then he is thinking about adding some type of tariffs to their products coming into the U.S.

President Trump has also increased tariffs on lumber and dairy products from Canada.

A *TARIFF* is a tax imposed on imported goods and services. Tariffs (value-added taxes) are used to restrict trade, as they increase the price of imported goods and services, making them more expensive to U.S. consumers. Among the likeliest would be special tariffs or other barriers to reduce the U.S. trade deficit with Mexico and tariffs (new taxes) that would encourage U.S. firms that relocated production there to return to the U.S., according to President Trump's advisers.

How Big is California's Economy (GDP)?
(In Trillions)

1. United States $17,947,000
2. China $11,007,721
3. Japan $4,123,258
4. Germany $3,357,614
5. United Kingdom $2,849,345
6. **California $2,424,033**
7. France $2,421,560
8. India $2,090,706
9. Italy $1,815,757
10. Brazil $1,772,589

The Importance of California Seaports

California seaports are a major economic force and are critically important to the growth of California and the nation's economy. Seaports are dependent upon the efficient movement of freight around the globe and across the nation.

The Ports of Los Angeles and Long Beach comprise the largest port complex in the United States and are key players in global enterprise. Together, they handle a fourth of all container cargo traffic in the United States. The Port of Oakland, the fourth largest port in the nation, handles trade from the Pacific Rim countries, delivering 99% of the ocean containers passing through Northern California and then transferred to trains and trucks for shipment to the rest of the nation.

California has 11 Pacific ports, which include 3 "megaports" (Los Angeles, Long Beach, and Oakland); 8 smaller niche ports (Hueneme, Humboldt Bay, Redwood City, Richmond, West Sacramento, San Diego, San Francisco, and Stockton); and 1 private port (Benicia). The ports of Oakland, Stockton, and West Sacramento are developing a new barge shipping service.

C. CALIFORNIA'S FUTURE GROWTH SECTORS

1. High Technology
2. Professional Services
3. Tourism and Entertainment
4. Foreign Trade

These are California's high-growth sectors for the next decade. Focus your attention on these sectors because they are growing faster than the U. S. economy.

Manufacturing is weak—regulations are causing firms to relocate.

Products and digital technologies in multimedia, telecommunications, and the use of the Internet symbolize the state's leadership position in future growth industries. California already has the economic base that other regions and nations are striving to create.

D. CALIFORNIA IS EXPERIENCING A JOB RECOVERY

Los Angeles and San Francisco have been experiencing slower job growth until now.

Chapman University economist and forecaster Jim Doti predicted that the California boom would be exceedingly concentrated in one region.

"It's not a California phenomenon, but a Silicon Valley job growth miracle, because the rest of the state really isn't doing well."

College students are not taking enough of the type of courses that may lead to jobs that are in demand.

The tech sector has also provided a huge portion of the state's specialized job volatility. Jobs expand greatly in good times, but decrease greatly in down times. There is no reason to believe that the tech sector's economic volatility has lessened.

Job Growth for California?

According to a recent UCLA Anderson Forecast, California should expect continued job growth and reduced unemployment figures over the next three years as the overall U.S. economy starts to pick up steam. The forecast calls for steady gains in employment from now through 2020. Payrolls are also expected to grow at about the current rate over the next three years.

The increase in U.S. growth rates from construction, automobiles, and business investment, combined with higher consumer demand, will continue to fuel our local economy.

California's employment should continue to grow faster than the U.S.

Real personal income growth in California is estimated to continue to be 3.7 percent or higher.

E. CALIFORNIA'S SLOW POPULATION GROWTH

Based on current slow growth estimates, the population of California will be between 40 and 41 million in 2020.

The population in California has passed 39,849,872 (12.5% of the U.S. population). Natural increase (the excess of births over deaths) and immigration will continue to be the key drivers of this growth. The foreign-born population will grow slightly faster than the U.S.-born population. By 2025, it is estimated that 30 percent of the state's residents will be foreign-born.

Over the next two decades, the population in California is projected to increase by 48% in lower cost inland counties (mostly Republicans), compared to 17% in coastal counties (mostly Democrats).

Projections show the fastest growth rates will be in the Inland Empire (Riverside and San Bernardino Counties), the San Joaquin Valley, and the Sacramento metropolitan area. Despite these uneven growth rates, 62% of the state's residents will still live in coastal counties in 2040.

Historical California Population		
Census	**Population**	**Percent ±**
1850	92,597	—
1860	379,994	310.4%
1870	560,247	47.4%
1880	864,694	54.3%
1890	1,213,398	40.3%
1900	1,485,053	22.4%
1910	2,377,549	60.1%
1920	3,426,861	44.1%
1930	5,677,251	65.7%
1940	6,907,387	21.7%
1950	10,586,223	53.3%
1960	15,717,204	48.5%
1970	19,953,134	27.0%
1980	23,667,902	18.6%
1990	29,760,021	25.7%
2000	33,871,684	13.8%
2010	37,253,956	10.0%
2015	38,715,000	10.0%
2016	39,497,345	0.90%
2017	39,849,872 (est.)	0.89%

Source: 2010 Census, California Department of Finance, and World Population Review

F. HISPANIC/LATINO POPULATION IS NOW THE LARGEST ETHNIC GROUP IN CALIFORNIA

Officially, Latinos and Hispanics outnumber the caucasian population in California.

Today over 50% of all Californians are Asian, Black, or Hispanic.

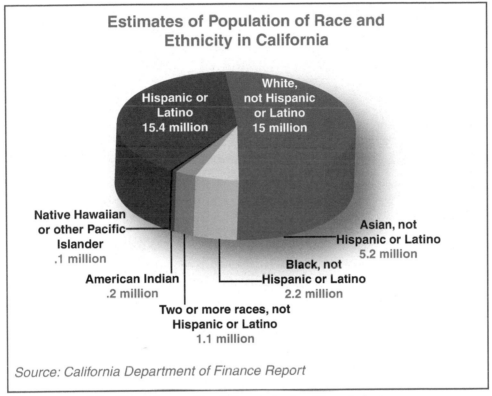

Estimates of Population of Race and Ethnicity in California

White, not Hispanic or Latino — 15 million

Hispanic or Latino — 15.4 million

Asian, not Hispanic or Latino — 5.2 million

Black, not Hispanic or Latino — 2.2 million

Two or more races, not Hispanic or Latino — 1.1 million

American Indian — .2 million

Native Hawaiian or other Pacific Islander — .1 million

Source: California Department of Finance Report

III. Facing California's Problems and Challenges

A. K-12 EDUCATION IS STILL SUFFERING

California still needs to build new classrooms or remodel old schools in certain areas.

Kindergarten through 12th grade education has suffered because of California's continuous population growth in lower income areas. There are so many students that education is one of the largest expenses for our state and county governments. Even though California has increased its educational spending to 42% of the state's annual budget, we still only rank 30th in the nation in per-child education spending.

K-12 Enrollment		
Ethnicity	**Number of Students**	**% of Total Enrollment**
Hispanic or Latino of Any Race	3,321,274	53.25%
American Indian/Alaska Native, Not Hispanic	36,755	0.62%
Asian, Not Hispanic	545,720	8.70%
Pacific Islander, Not Hispanic	31,513	0.53%
Filipino, Not Hispanic	158,224	2.43%
African American, Not Hispanic	373,280	6.16%
White, Not Hispanic	1,531,088	25.00%
Two or More Races, Not Hispanic	175,700	2.68%
None Reported	38,809	0.63%
Total	**6,235,520**	**100.00%**

Source: California Department of Education
www.cde.ca.gov/ds/sd/cb/ceffingertipfacts.asp

There has been a slowdown overall in the total number of school children. However, because California did not keep up when the population was rapidly growing, we have never recovered and still have a high demand in lower income areas for classrooms, textbooks, and teachers.

While most other countries that require excellence in K-12 grades, California also focuses on excellence in college work and creates opportunities for anyone who attends college and chooses a relevant major. California's biggest downfall is that many students fall through the cracks in the K-12 grades and are not prepared to go on to college. At this time, our system does not provide good vocational alternatives for such students.

Educational attainment levels will continue to increase in the state. Among all of the state's racial/ethnic groups, California's overall population appears to be shifting toward groups that tend to have lower levels of education. Projections of the state's economy

The Cost of Higher Education

The University of California has approved its first tuition increase in six years as a result of enrollment growth and a reduction in state support that left universities unable to pay for more faculty, courses, and financial aid. Annual tuition for in-state students would rise by more than $300; nonresidents would face a total yearly increase of $1,668.

Under the proposal, tuition would grow to $11,502 for the 2017-18 school year—a 2.5% increase of $282. The student services fee would increase to $1,128, a $54 increase. But financial aid would cover the increases for two-thirds of the university's California resident students, who number about 175,500.

Nonresident undergraduates would face a total increase of $1,668. They would pay the same increases in base tuition and student fees but also a 5% hike in their supplemental tuition, which would rise $1,332—from $26,682 currently to $28,014 next year.

One solution to the growing cost of higher education (and the accompanying debt) is attending community college before transferring to the university system.

suggest that employers will require even more college graduates than the state's population seems likely to supply. Population projections suggest that by 2020, 33% of 25-64 year olds will have a college degree, but projections of the state's economy suggest that demand for specific college graduates will be even higher (39% of all workers).

1. Higher Education is Excellent

In California we hear a lot about our K-12 schools struggling for more money, increased space, better high school graduation rates, and achievement test scores, but this certainly does not apply to California's colleges.

California colleges are not only the envy of the United States but also the rest of the world, which sends its sons and daughters here to study.

There are over 113 community colleges in California with enrollment of well over two million students. This constitutes about 25% of America's community college students who obtain a two-year degree.

Our California State University and University of California systems are highly ranked and still relatively inexpensive for residents of our state. Even with occasional increases in tuition, higher education is still a bargain in California.

California's community colleges and universities have the largest total number of students enrolled in the nation.

2. How Student Loans Drive Up Debt

Why is student loan debt increasing? It is partly due to the fact that as tuitions grow higher, more and more students are forced to take out student loans to pay for school as well as rent, food, car payments, and living expenses. Unfortunately, it's a vicious cycle; as more students get loans, more money floods the schools—encouraging universities and colleges to invest in more elaborate facilities for students and higher pay for professors, employees, board of trustee members, and administrators.

Because student loans cannot be discharged by bankruptcy, they follow students forever—often forcing them to live at home longer or in substandard conditions due to the crushing debt they owe. This decreases their contributions to the state revenues (homes sales, for example).

The more students who enroll in college, the more instructors must be hired, and their seeming success rate at raising enrollment makes them feel entitled to higher salaries. In addition, the incoming money from student loans drives the need to build more elaborate student centers, attain more expensive furnishings, remodel, and upgrade buildings and high-tech access. More students also means more parking—and well-groomed campuses.

This tendency also increases contractors' incentives to build expensive rental units for "seemingly" privileged students—the rent for which only contributes to the need for more student loans and increasing inability to pay them off in a reasonable period of time after graduation.

All of this "unforgivable" debt ties the hands of the borrowers who could be contributing to the wealth of the state, but instead are busy paying the national government who supplies the majority of student loans. Something must be done; the question is what?

Facts About California Community Colleges

- California Community Colleges have the highest rate of public attendance of all community college systems in the nation (2.1 million students).

- One-quarter of all community college students nationwide are enrolled in a California Community College.

- Three out of every ten Californians age 18-24 are currently enrolled in a Community College.

Source: Foundation for California Community Colleges

B. CONGESTED FREEWAYS, ROADS, AND POTHOLES

1. Better Transportation is Needed

Each day there are 1,000 more cars on California roads.

Although voters have tried to fix our crumbling roads and infrastructure through the proposition process, this requires the issuance of billions of dollars in bonds. It's never really enough to fix the ongoing problem.

Road problems cost the average California motorist $762 a year in repair costs, according to a study from TRIP, a Washington, D.C.-based transportation research organization. And none of the 20 most critical transportation projects in the Los Angeles area—including regular highway maintenance, expansion of the Metro Purple Line, or expanding Interstate 405—has enough funding available.

California's reliance on gas taxes in the past to repair its transportation network is becoming less and less tenable. Increased fuel economy standards have led to less spending on gasoline—a process the state is trying to speed up through its climate change goals by encouraging people to drive less and buy electric cars.

Governor Jerry Brown increased gas taxes 12 cents per gallon and instituted higher car registration fees by a whopping 42% in 2017, implying it was for repairing roads and potholes. In reality, this law requires the money be spent on "transportation projects,"which could include trains, real estate for rail tracks, electric charging stations, and airports. Many from the inland counties and cities will be hit hardest because these hard-working people need to travel longer distances. If the money does not go to repair roads, it will be unfair to many.

Are California and President Trump in a War?

Will California's share of the infrastructure budget suffer because of our state's antagonistic attitude towards Trump?

Rehabbing America's aging infrastructure is a Trump priority and possible the biggest job Elaine Chao, Donald Trump's Secretary of Transportation, will have.

 Trump said, "We are going to fix our inner cities and rebuild our highways, bridges, tunnels, and airports. We're going to rebuild our infrastructure, which will become, by the way, second to none."

It could be one of the least controversial things he said on the trail.

According to the Federal Highway Safety Administration, nearly 10 percent of America's bridges, about 60,000, are classified as deficient, and the American Society of Civil Engineers says 32 percent of our major roads are in poor or mediocre condition. AAA estimates that potholes alone cost American drivers $3 billion a year. The Federal Aviation Administration says airport congestion and flight delays cost the country more than $31 billion annually.

Trump pledged to spend up to "$1 trillion" on transportation and infrastructure over the next decade.

The infusion of cash would be spurred by billions in tax credits for construction companies, which would be later repaid through income taxes on contractor profits and taxes on wages earned by the workers.

The White House—led by the self-proclaimed building expert —would focus on finishing projects on time and under budget. This would presumably be done by streamlining the permit process and eliminating wasteful spending.

Critics say this is just another tax crisis—that adds to California's already high tax burden that "caused" California's abnormally slow growth and its shrinking labor force for over a decade.

C. CALIFORNIA'S POVERTY "INEQUALITY" IS EXPANDING

California is home to over 30% of U.S. welfare recipients and 20.6% of Californians are living in poverty. No doubt this is due to our cost of living—the highest rate in the country.

A Pew Research Center study found that California's urban areas are among the regions where the middle class is shrinking the most rapidly.

How can this be, in light of new job growth? You have to look at the kind of jobs being created. Over the last decade, nearly all the high-wage, blue-collar sectors (manufacturing, construction, energy and natural resources) have declined, even as the rest of the country experienced a resurgence in energy and manufacturing.

California's "comeback" is misleading, as the state's poverty and financial inequality levels are rising.

D. HOME PRICES AND RENTS (Extremely Expensive)

Housing in California is so expensive that most households are forced to make serious trade-offs in order to live. Should you pay high rents for a small unit near work or pay less and commute a longer distance?

Living in decent, affordable, and reasonably located housing is vitally important to every Californian. Unfortunately, housing in California is extremely expensive and, as a result, many households are forced to make serious trade-offs, such as where we work and live, in order to remain here.

While many factors contribute to California's high housing costs, the most important is the significant shortage of housing in the state's highly coveted coastal communities.

California's cost-of-living is higher than most other states.

California's rents, averaging $2,050 for a two-bedroom unit, are about 50 percent above the national average.

Three California cities (San Francisco, San Jose, and Los Angeles) are among the nation's 10 highest-cost cities, with San Francisco number one at $4,690 average per month rent for a two-bedroom unit.

California: Highest Poverty Rate in US

With 39.8 million residents, the Census Bureau has reported that 8.9 million of California's population lives in poverty!

It may seem unrealistic, but the wealthiest state in the nation has a whopping 20.6 percent poverty rate. The highest rate in California is Los Angeles at 26.9 percent, followed by Napa at 25.5 percent. It comes as a surprise to many that some of the highest poverty rates in the state are in the San Francisco Bay Area and coastal communities, which are usually considered very affluent because of their high cost of housing.

Techno-wealth has led to the death of the middle class in many wealthy communities.

The reasoning behind this phenomenon is debatable, but many political analysts believe this anomaly is due to the fact that the "wealthy coastal elite," who make their money in high technology digital industries, drive up the cost of living (high rents) in these areas. The economy has shifted so dramatically in favor of the wealthy "information age" elitists that they have made it difficult or impossible for the middle class to make a living in their communities. (See Chapter 7 for more information.)

The crisis is with 15 million Californians who live in poverty or what the Public Policy Institute of California calls "near-poverty." Unfortunately, it is common for families in major urban areas to devote well over 50 percent of their meager incomes to shelter.

California's housing costs are highest in cities, such as San Francisco, that tend to be the most liberal politically, and local resistance to construction in those cities, in the name of environmental protection, is also the most intense.

The ever-widening gap between the housing that California needs to keep pace with its modest increases in population, but the lack of construction has driven rents through the roof.

1. Lack of Housing and New Construction

Due to the lack of new housing construction, the so called "tech boom" is being undermined by brutally high home prices and expensive rents.

Only 13 percent of San Franciscans can purchase the county's median home at standard interest rates.

In San Mateo, only 16 percent can qualify to purchase a house. It is no surprise that as many as "one in three" Bay Area residents and businesses are now thinking of leaving the region.

There are clear signs that job growth in the Bay Area is slowing as companies look for space in less expensive, less highly regulated areas of the state or country.

Established tech companies now suggest that new startup companies may be financially better off launching somewhere else because of high priced real estate (i.e., offices and employee homes).

2. The Real Estate Lending Crash Stopped Construction

At one time, California had issued 205,000 housing permits a year. But as the loan bubble burst, activity dropped (in 2009) to as low as 35,000 before beginning a slow rise again. During the same period, California's population rose by 3 million.

California was part of the housing market crash but housing prices have recovered while construction of new units has not.

Today the average household size in California is 2.78 persons, which indicates we need over 1.2 million new units to be built because of the backlog.

Handling California's affordable housing shortage is one of the state's biggest challenges. There must be a change in the state's priorities, including tax structure and spending options, to deal with the growing need for affordable living space that will continue into the next decade. The real challenge is not how to stop population growth but how to keep jobs in the state by providing an affordable cost of living.

E. AIR QUALITY AND TRANSPORTATION

Although air quality has improved over several decades, smog, the long-time air problem of Los Angeles, has spread over a large portion of Southern California. With 1,000 more cars on the road each day, it is no wonder that the southern part of the state has serious air quality problems. The cherished car is causing most of the problems. Organizations with over 100 employees must regulate hours, encourage car pooling, and utilize electric cars, according to the **Air Quality Management District (AQMD)**, the organization responsible for the area's air quality standards.

TRUMP ANXIETY

Among President Trump's executive orders are two that would allow oil and gas drilling on all federal lands and in coastal waters, although they will possibly face years of reviews. Californians: Do you realize that **forty-five percent** of all California land is owned by the federal government? Also, six California national monuments designated by former administrations are called a "land grab" by President Trump. He wants to give these monuments back to our state.

F. CALIFORNIA IS UNFRIENDLY TO BUSINESS

1. Texas has Replaced California as a Job Growth State

Economically, California is behind Texas. California is barely growing jobs because of our high cost of living. Over the last decade, Texas has taken over our position as the top creator of:

1. jobs,
2. households, and
3. population growth.

Comparing California to Texas, job growth rates in Austin and Dallas have been higher than that in the Bay Area, while Los Angeles has lagged well behind.

Since the turn of this century, the Texas capital of Austin has increased its jobs by over 50 percent, while Raleigh, Houston, San Antonio, Dallas, Nashville, Orlando, Charlotte, Phoenix, and Salt Lake City— cities all in lower-tax, regulation-light states—have seen job growth of 24 percent or above.

California and its cities are some of the highest taxed and regulated, resulting in sub-par job growth.

2. Our Legislature is Too Anti-Business

California is the 49th-ranked state in business climate.

A history of pro-union and anti-business sentiment only served to hurt employers, employees, and the California economy. One reason a state with so many advantages suffered such a large negative economic decline was because of bad government decisions made over a number of years.

Although the leader in so many business arenas, like high-technology, foreign trade, tourism and entertainment, professional services, and diversified manufacturing, the state could not withstand the assault of so much anti-business legislation for long. Some of those regulations resulted in:

1. The second highest personal income tax rate in the nation.
2. One of the highest corporate tax rates in the nation.
3. The second highest electricity rates in the nation.
4. Overly complex, costly, and time-consuming business regulations.
5. One of the worst workers' compensation systems in the nation.
6. Sales taxes well above the national average.
7. 50th in spending per capita on highways.
8. Overdue water projects.
9. Inadequate K-12 school facilities.
10. 32% higher cost of unemployment insurance.

G. CALIFORNIA'S TAXES HIGHEST IN NATION

Jerry Brown did well in California's eight-year budget recovery—while quietly saying he even put $2 billion extra in the reserves in case of a potential recession.

Cities and counties currently run an unfunded public employee pension liability (debt) of $1 trillion, along with what the State Controller says is more like a $1.5 trillion debt.

In the 2016 November General Election, over $500 billion in new taxes and bond measures passed. Has California voted itself into future recession and bankruptcy?

The state's current budget surplus is entirely due to higher tax rates and an increase in tax revenue coming from the sale of higher priced real estate. **The top 1 percent of earners generates almost half of California's income tax revenue, and accounts for 41 percent of the state's general fund budget**. These affluent people have incomes that are much more closely correlated to rising stock and real estate prices than state economic activity. But remember: these stocks and bonds values are more volatile than economic activity generally. Brown's own Department of Finance

California:
Fight for Economic Survival

The Mexican-American War of 1846-1848 resulted in Texas and California becoming part of the United States. Despite our common origin, and the many things our states share in common, our current political and economic points of view are drifting further and further apart. When Rick Perry was still governor of Texas (a **RED STATE**, *meaning predominantly Republican*), he visited California (a **BLUE STATE**, *meaning predominantly Democrat*) to lure away businesses and jobs, signaling more than a rivalry between these two mega-states. The Texas-California competition represents the political, economic, and cultural differences driving American politics today—and for the foreseeable future.

Texas and California are robust political and economic competitors.

California is a global hub for trade, tourism, culture, and the manufacture of ideas and intellectual property. From high-tech and biotech to entertainment, travel and logistics, the state's "brand" transcends national boundaries. The Golden State tops the nation in agriculture. It also sets the pace on "green energy" development, which has led to costly increases in the state's energy production.

The Texas economy, too, has always been based on energy and agriculture. But it has been building a manufacturing and service base, and as a "red state" attracting businesses with lower wage rates, weaker unions, a friendly regulatory climate, and large fiscal incentives. California and Texas are political opposites.

The two states are most sharply divided by their very different "cultural, economic and political" values.

Governor Brown's Prop 30 (raising state income and sales taxes) has disgruntled California entrepreneurs, corporate executives, and workers looking for a more business-friendly atmosphere.

Former Governor Rick Perry's "dissing" of California's economy and business policies also resonates with the Golden State's GOP primary voters, whose mantra is that the sky has fallen because

Democrats and unions are now holding all the political cards. In the debate over which state has the economic edge, both sides have their talking points. Texas has lower taxes, less unemployment and an energy boom—as well as a lower minimum wage. California leads in venture capital and in the innovation and creativity recognized the world over as unique to Hollywood and the Silicon Valley.

California's Pacific Rim ports also provide a strategic advantage for trade. The mega-ports of Los Angeles, Long Beach, and Oakland are ranked in the top 25 world ports. Our sunny Mediterranean climate is also a huge draw, as well as the intangibles of glamour and lifestyle. With the enlargement of the Panama Canal, Texas ports will create thousands of jobs. Texas can also boast of lower housing costs and a more business-friendly regulatory system. What both states share are the huge burdens of handling infrastructure and environmental challenges.

Thanks to Prop. 13, California has lower property taxes (only 1%) than Texas, but it's still cheaper to buy property in Texas than in California. In addition to higher income taxes in California, businesses complain about the state's slow, burdensome regulatory process, litigious overkill, the confounding layers of government, the out-sized political power of public employee unions, and the devastating results of those public unions' unfunded pensions.

One of California's biggest economic drivers has traditionally been its strong educational system. But public higher education has been under the budgetary gun in recent years.

A quarter of all Texans have bachelor's degrees, while roughly a third of Californians do, which could be due to the fact that California has twice as many community colleges as Texas, offering the first step towards earning a degree. Both states are struggling with K-12 funding and the challenge of educating a large immigrant population.

Why is this rivalry between states important? Because without a new "gold rush" (fracking anyone?) California may experience a "corporation rush" out of the state and into Texas!

predicts that a recession of "average magnitude" would cut revenue by over $55 billion.

H. CALIFORNIA'S FINANCES RELY ON DEBT!

Governor Brown is forecasting budget deficits of $4 billion by the time he leaves office in 2019.

California is one of the states that is most deeply dependent on debt. California's fiscal performance is weak across several categories.

In the long run, California is too heavily reliant on borrowing money to pay for expenses! Particularly concerning is the massive teacher and public employees' pension fund deficit that could consume our state finances in the near future.

When valued on a guaranteed-to-be-paid basis, California's teacher and instructor (**California State Teachers' Retirement System - CalSTRS**) and public employees (**California Public Employees' Retirement System - CalPERS**) unfunded pension liabilities are $756 billion and health care benefits are $29 billion. This unfunded debt is rapidly growing.

Face it: California has a "trillion dollars-plus" in unfunded teacher and public employee pension liabilities (debt) that we are not paying down!

More financial pension details are explained in Chapter 9 and 10.

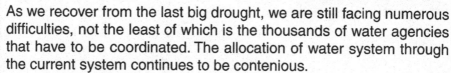

California's Most Precious Resource... Water

Water allocation and Project Management:

1. Continuous water shortages
2. Ground water pollution
3. Arizona is taking more from the Colorado River
4. Erratic weather patterns

As we recover from the last big drought, we are still facing numerous difficulties, not the least of which is the thousands of water agencies that have to be coordinated. The allocation of water system through the current system continues to be contenious.

Everybody wants more water!

IV. Chapter Summary

President Trump lost California's popular vote by 4.2 million and also lost 55 electoral college votes.

California has a **supermajority** (two-thirds) in the state legislature. This means the Democrat-controlled state legislature (Assembly and Senate) can pass certain legislation with a two-thirds vote, regardless of how the Republicans vote.

California's high tech digital corporations, with their highly educated employees, are making lots of money. Meanwhile, middle-income workers who, in the past, prospered in manufacturing have been pushed out because of punishing regulations. Finally, those with lower incomes and fewer skills find it hard to survive (shamefully 20.6% live below the poverty line).

Governor Brown has tried to persuade voters to support ballot initiatives that asked voters to raise taxes on themselves.

If ranked as its own country, **California would be the 6th largest economy in the world, based on Gross Domestic Product (GDP)**.

California is a world class economic power because it is economically diverse. **Economic diversity** means that many economic activities are balanced so that no one industry dominates to the extent that, if eliminated, it would cause severe problems. Economic power is measured by gross domestic product. **Gross Domestic Product (GDP)** is the sum of all products and services produced by a country in a given year.

Trade is clearly one of the driving industries in California. Between exports and imports, California has boosted jobs in air transportation, wholesale trades, and port facilities. **Exports** are manufactured goods, agricultural produce, minerals, and other items produced in the United States but purchased by other countries. Our top seven export partners are: Mexico, Japan, Canada, China, South Korea, United Kingdom, and Taiwan. **Imports** are goods and services purchased from other countries.

California's future growth sectors should include high technology, foreign trade, tourism and entertainment, professional services, and diversified manufacturing.

California's population has grown to over 39,800,000 (12.5% of the U.S. population). There is no single ethic or racial majority group in California, although over 50% of the population is now Hispanic, Asian, or Black.

Over the next two decades, the population in California is projected to increase by 48% in inland counties, compared to 17% in coastal counties. Projections show the fastest growth rates will be in the Inland Empire (Riverside and San Bernardino Counties), the San Joaquin Valley, and the Sacramento metropolitan area.

Kindergarten through 12th grade education has had to make adjustments because of California's continuous secondary language population growth. Education is one of the largest expenses for our state and county governments. Even though California has increased its educational spending to 42% of the state's annual budget, we still only rank 30th in the nation in per-child education spending.

There are over 113 community colleges in California with enrollment of well over two million students.

With 1,000 more cars on the road each day due to California's increasing population, it is no wonder that the southern part of the state has serious air quality problems.

Housing in California is so extremely expensive that most households are forced to make serious trade-offs in order to live. Should you pay high rents for a small unit near work or pay less ans commute a longer distance?

California relies too heavily on income taxes. **The top one percent of earners generates almost half of California's income tax revenue, and accounts for 41 percent of the state's general fund budget.**

California owes too much money. California has a "trillion dollar-plus" in unfunded teacher and public employee pension liabilities (debt) that we are not paying down!

V. Class Discussion Questions

1. What is the status of California's population growth?
2. What can be done about congested freeways, roads, and potholes?
3. In what ways is our legislature too anti-business?
4. How is California too reliant on debt?

Chapter 2

Early California History and the Federal Government

I. Early California History

A. NATIVE AMERICANS

Native Americans numbered about 150,000 before the Europeans started coming in large numbers to California. The moderate climate and abundant food supply sustained the 135 loosely organized tribes. At one time one-eighth of all indigenous Indian Tribes lived in California.

The white man greatly contributed to the decline of the Indian population through the introduction of diseases (small pox, malaria, venereal disease), manufactured Indian wars, and the destruction of their food supplies. By 1900 there were only about 16,000 Native Americans remaining in California.

B. UNDER THE FLAG OF SPAIN

In 1542, on a voyage paralleling the California coast, Juan Rodriquez Cabrillo sailed into San Diego Bay and named it "San Miguel." Although the name did not survive, Cabrillo is credited with being the first European to land in what is now known as California. The Spanish established settlements along the California coastline. These settlements were linked when the mission system was created.

Chapter Outline

C. CALIFORNIA MISSIONS

Father Junipero Serra is recognized as the first real colonizer of California. Father Serra, a Catholic Franciscan Priest from Spain, established the first mission (1769) near what is now downtown San Diego. The second mission, near Monterey Bay, is where Father Serra is buried. Spain used four types of settlements to colonize California: missions, presidios, pueblos, and ranchos.

The **MISSIONS** *were Spanish-style adobe buildings with high arches, long corridors, and red tiled roofs that surrounded a courtyard.* Missions were created for more than religious instruction. They were similar to vocational schools where the natives could learn a trade and how to care for farms and orchards. Father Serra personally established nine missions, the number later growing to 21.

PRESIDIOS *were frontier forts.* Most were located at strategic locations, usually at the entrance to a pueblo or port. **PUEBLOS** *were clusters of adobe houses, usually including a church, that formed a town or small city.* Among the first settlements were San Jose in 1777 and Los Angeles, "the City of the Angels," in 1781.

EL CAMINO REAL *is Spanish for "The King's Highway." It is the original horseback trail used to travel between missions and from presidio to presidio.* The missions were located so that they were only a day's horseback ride from each other. Bells on a staff-shaped post now mark these routes and are often seen on US Route 1 while traveling along the California coast.

D. MEXICAN RULE: 1821-1846

Mexico won its independence from Spain in 1821.

Historical note: Mexico repelled a French invasion force on May 5, 1862. **CINCO de MAYO (Fifth of May)** *marks the date of the battle (not Mexican Independence Day) with the French in which Mexico turned back its first foreign invader as an independent country.* Cinco de Mayo is more widely celebrated in the U.S. as a celebration of Mexican-American culture.

In 1833, under the **Mexican Secularization Act,** Mexico seized the missions and the surrounding lands. They then distributed half the land to the California Indians. The missions were stripped of their lands and converted into parish churches.

California's Political/ Historical Timeline

SUMMARY OF IMPORTANT HISTORICAL DATES

1500 – Native Indians who first inhabited the land numbered 150,000 before the white man introduced his diseases and prejudice.

1540 – Sea expedition led by Hernando de Alarcon up Gulf of California to mouth of Colorado River.

1542 – Juan Rodriguez Cabrillo discovered San Diego—considered to be the first European to set foot in California—only 50 years after Columbus discovered "America." He also discovered Catalina Islands, sites of San Pedro and Santa Monica and Santa Barbara Channel Islands.

1579 – Sir Francis Drake landed north of San Francisco Bay, claimed the territory for England.

1669 – Gaspar de Portola, governor of the Californias, led an expedition up the Pacific coast, established California's first mission on San Diego Bay.

1769 – Father Junipero Serra began establishing the first nine of 21 Missions from San Diego to Sonoma, each a one-day horseback ride apart.

1821 – Mexico won its independence from Spain in 1821.

1827 – Jedediah Smith, the first American to cross the Sierra Mountains, arrived in California.

1848 – Gold was discovered by James Marshall near Sacramento at Sutter's sawmill. "Eureka" (I have found it) – the gold rush was on.

1848 – Treaty of Guadalupe Hidalgo – Mexico officially ceded California to the United States.

1849 – California's first constitution.

1850 – California is admitted to the Union as the 31st state on September 9,1850.

1869 – Transcontinental railroad completed – The Southern Pacific Railroad continued its growth and monopolistic practices; later it became known as the "Octopus."

1880 – California adopted its second constitution, restricting Chinese employment, railroads, and corporate officials.

1906 – San Francisco earthquake killed 3,000, left 225,000 homeless.

1910 – Angel Island opened, entry point to U. S. for immigrants.

1911 – An amendment to the State Constitution gave us the tools of direct democracy: recall, referendum, and initiative.

1911 – Women won right to vote.

1933 – Long Beach earthquake caused widespread damage throughout southern California; Alcatraz made a prison.

1936 – San Francisco-Oakland Bay Bridge opened.

1936 – Golden Gate Bridge completed.

1936 – Parker Dam completed.

1942 – Internment during World II of Japanese-American citizens.

1945 – United Nations Charter signed in San Francisco.

1978 – Proposition 13 passed by voters. This property tax limitation initiative helped overtaxed homeowners, but greatly restricted county government.

1988 – Proposition 98 mandated that at least 40% of general funds must go to K-12 and community colleges.

1989 – 7.1 magnitude earthquake hit Bay Area.

1990 – Proposition 140 passed. This term limitation initiative reduced the number of terms that a state legislator could serve and lessened their staffs and pensions.

1994 – Proposition 187 limited public services that could be offered to illegal aliens.

2000 – Electricity crisis caused blackouts and large rate increases.

2003 – For the first time, California recalled its governor, Gray Davis, Arnold Schwarzenegger became governor.

2011 – Jerry Brown becomes governor for the second time (reelected in 2015).

2011 – Illegal immigrants allowed to receive state aid for college.

2016 - Marijuana legalized.

2016 - Death Penalty reaffirmed.

2016 - Donald Trump elected President—how will he treat California?

At the same time, some select, wealthy gentlemen established ranchos. The *RANCHOS were large parcels of land given to families of prominence to establish large, un-fenced grazing areas for raising cattle.* Between 1830 and 1845, the number of private ranchos on land grants increased from 50 to 1,045.

E. CALIFORNIA IS TAKEN FROM MEXICO

The Bear Flag Revolt started in California on June 14, 1846, before anyone realized that the United States had already declared war on Mexico. The *BEAR FLAG REVOLT started over the fear that the Mexican government would move against settlers in California.* The revolt began in Sonoma where General Marino Guadalupe Vallejo was put under house arrest by a band of American settlers who declared an independent "Republic of California." A symbol of this battle was a flag with a bear gazing at a single star. The motto on the flag read:

> **"A bear stands his ground always, and as long as the stars shine we stand for the cause."**

The Bear Flag Revolt was a short-lived event. It ended 22 days later when Mexico surrendered control of Monterey to U.S. forces.

The United States had declared war on Mexico in 1846 over a boundary dispute in Texas. By 1847, U.S. Troops had control of Texas, New Mexico, Arizona, and California. The United States and Mexico signed the Treaty of Guadalupe Hidalgo on February 2, 1848. The *TREATY OF GUADALUPE HIDALGO ended the war with Mexico and allowed the California Republic to become part of the United States.* The treaty honored the earlier Spanish land grants and later Mexican land grants.

F. GOLD WAS DISCOVERED

On January 24, 1848, gold was discovered by James Wilson Marshall, a carpenter employed by John Sutter to construct a sawmill at Coloma on a branch of the American River. The sound of "Eureka!" was heard around the world. *EUREKA refers to the gold rush and means "I have found it!"*

The greatest influx of gold hunters was in 1849, hence the new arrivals were given the name "forty-niners." Hysteria about the amount of gold caused California's population to swell, especially around Sacramento, from 15,000 in 1848, to over 92,000 by 1850 and again to 380,000 by 1860. But even after the gold fever broke, people continued to come. The completion of the transcontinental railroad (1869) continued to bring

California Republic Flag

Current California Flag

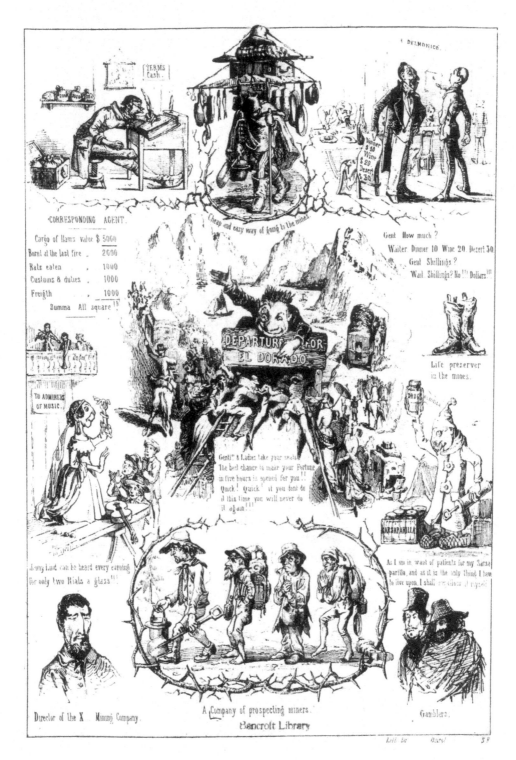

Engraved by Charles H. Holmes, of Sacramento, in 1888; copied from an old print in an early California magazine.

California Capitol Building at San Jose – 1849-1851

more people to establish or work in merchandising and manufacturing companies.

G. CALIFORNIA STATEHOOD: 1850

In the Fall of 1849, a constitutional convention was held, and the new Californians overwhelmingly approved their first California Constitution. It established a state government that is similar to today's state government.

The California constitution included:

1. Bill of Rights (in the beginning)
2. Plural executive branch
3. Legislature (Senate and Assembly)
4. Elected judicial branch (four levels of courts—now three levels)
5. White males 21 years of age could vote
6. Government documents were printed in English and Spanish

The U.S. Congress approved this constitution and California became the 31st state admitted to the Union. *ADMISSION DAY is September 9, 1850, the date California became a state.* There was much concern as to whether California would be admitted as a slave or free state, but the U.S. Congress moved very quickly to make California another non-slave state for the Union.

H. THE GREAT SEAL OF THE STATE OF CALIFORNIA

The constitutional convention of 1849 adopted the **"Great Seal of the State of California."** Around the top of the ring are 31 stars representing California's position as the 31st state admitted to the Union. The foreground figure represents the Goddess Minerva who, according to Greek mythology, sprang full-grown from the head of Zeus, her father. She symbolizes the political birth of the state of California without having to go through the probation of being a territory. At her feet is a gold miner and also a grizzly bear feeding on grape vines. The snow-capped peaks of the Sierra Nevada are in the background with the state motto "Eureka," which refers to the gold rush.

The Secretary of State is the keeper of the Great Seal, which is used to emboss official state documents. A person who misuses or reproduces the Great Seal without permission is guilty of a misdemeanor.

I. THE RAILROADS (Good and Bad)

The Central Pacific Railroad Company's eventual founders were referred to as the "Big Four." Their last names may still sound familiar today:

Leland Stanford
Collis P. Huntington
Mark Hopkins
Charles Crocker

President Lincoln signed the **Pacific Railroad Bill (1862)** that called for the simultaneous start of the Central Pacific Railroad (later acquired by lease from the Southern Pacific Railroad) in Sacramento and Union Pacific Railroad in Omaha. The bill called for these two railroad lines to receive land and government subsidies based on the miles of rail laid. The extreme wealth and power of the big four railroad barons enabled them to gain a stranglehold on the early economic and political life of California. For 50 years (1860-1910), the railroads were the dominant economic force that shaped California's growth. Thousands of Chinese workers were brought to California to help build the railroads, working

The Great Seal of the State of California

under near-slavery conditions. The transcontinental railroad network was completed when the two railroads were joined by the famous "gold spike" at Promontory, Utah, in 1869.

But, in the 1890s, things changed for the **"octopus,"** the name given to the railroad companies. William Randolph Hearst, who inherited the San Francisco Examiner newspaper from his father, started an ongoing crusade against the Big Four by publishing critical articles and pointed political cartoons.

J. CALIFORNIA'S SECOND CONSTITUTION

The *WORKINGMEN'S PARTY was an anti-railroad group that disapproved of the large number of unemployed Chinese abandoned in the wake of the railroad construction.* Their reform measures, which were later approved by the state legislature, included: a public school system, an eight-hour work day, land monopoly laws, restrictions on Chinese labor, and laws defining the responsibility of corporate directors and officers. The movement was so strong that the *SECOND CALIFORNIA STATE CONSTITUTION (1879) was adopted and later ratified by the voters after a special constitutional convention.*

The "Octopus"

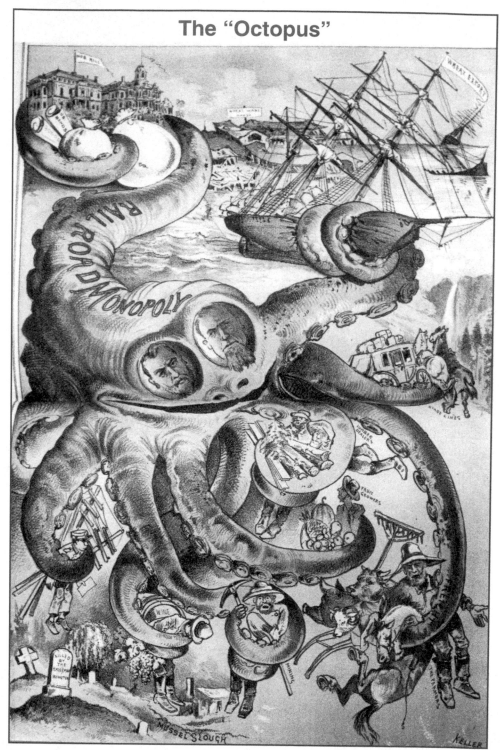

A *CONSTITUTIONAL CONVENTION is an accepted method to alter a state's constitution or to write an entirely new document, which is submitted to the electorate for a ratification vote.*

K. THE CALIFORNIA PROGRESSIVES (Reformers)

In the early part of the 20th century, the Southern Pacific Railroad (its new name) was still monopolizing California's politics and manipulating politicians. But the California Progressive Party changed this situation. The *PROGRESSIVES were a group of reform-minded Republicans who split from the party to enact permanent changes in the political system that are the basis of the election laws today.*

Hiram Johnson, the new Progressive governor, pushed for political reforms. Among the reform measures passed in 1911 were the: initiative, referendum, recall, direct primary, nonpartisan city and county elections, and a civil service system. The Progressives introduced direct democracy into the California political system. See Chapter 4 for more details.

II. The Federal Government: State vs. Federal Powers

In this part of the chapter we look at the two arenas in which California Politics unfolds. The **first arena** is California's representatives to the federal system: the U.S. Senate and the U.S. House of Representatives. We will also look at the Presidency of the United States. The rest of this chapter is devoted to how this federal system is played out on the California political stage and how the state gets money from the federal government.

The **second arena** is pure California: our governor and our state legislature.

A. CERTAIN POWERS ARE RESERVED FOR THE STATE

The highest source of power in the United States is the U.S. Constitution, but certain powers are reserved for the states. The **10th Amendment to the Constitution of the United States** reads:

> **"The powers not delegated to the United States by the Constitution, nor prohibited by it to the States, are reserved to the States respectively, or to the people."**

Among other powers reserved solely for the states are the powers to:

1. Establish and control local governments
2. Conduct elections
3. Allow for the formation of business corporations

4. Establish civil and criminal laws
5. Utilize police powers

Of the various powers reserved for the state, police power is probably one of the most important. *POLICE POWER permits the state to take action to protect the public health, safety, morals, and welfare of its citizens.*

Some powers are concurrent. *CONCURRENT POWERS are powers shared by both the state and the federal government.* Two very important concurrent powers are the ability to tax and to borrow money.

III. California's Money from Washington

In the last three decades the federal government has been giving money to the states and local governments to help with certain programs. These financial incentives are the federal government's way of influencing and coaxing each individual state to do what Washington, D.C. wants it to do. It is a way to redistribute taxes collected by the federal government to the states. In the 1960s, the federal government began sharing 15% of the nation's budget with the states and local governments, and by 1980, this figure had risen to an all-time high of 23%. **The method that the federal government uses to make money available and send to California is called grant-in-aid.**

Will President Trump attempt to influence a Republican-controlled U.S. Congress to withhold federal funds if we reject his agendas?

A. GRANT-IN-AID (Money Sent ot California)

GRANT-IN-AID is money given from one governmental body to another for a specific purpose. These grants come with strings attached from the U.S. Congress. Most grants require matching funds. *MATCHING FUNDS are federal monies given to the state or local governments that must be matched, dollar for dollar, or they will not be granted.*

Grant-in-aid is disbursed in two different ways: categorical grants and block grants. *CATEGORICAL GRANTS are grants made for a specific purpose or to target a specific program.* The restrictions of this type of grant leave the recipient with very little discretion. Two examples of categorical grants are programs for AIDS patients and the homeless.

The opposite of a categorical grant is a block grant. A *FEDERAL BLOCK GRANT is the awarding of money for general purposes from one level of government to another.* Of the 400 grants-in-aid available, only 14 are currently block grants. This type of grant allows the recipients the freedom to allocate the money among individual programs. For example, if a block grant is for mass transit, it can be used for buses, trains, or construction of stations.

Welfare, a state administered program, was a huge federal program, but now California must decide how best to direct it.

Many of these federal grant-in-aid programs have worked to remove gross inequities among the states. But remember—these programs are highly political. For example, the 1984 Highway Act reduced the amount of money available to states that allowed those under 21 years of age to consume alcoholic beverages. Within four years, every state in the union had a minimum drinking age of 21.

The Effect in California of President Trump's Proposed Disbursement of Federal Funds

President Trump's spending plan envisions deep cuts to many Cabinet departments and agencies. It will no doubt face opposition from both parties in Congress. The spending plan includes:

1. EPA	-31.4%
2. Foreign Aid	-28.7%
3. Agriculture	-20.7%
4. Labor	-20.7%
5. Health and Human Services	-16.2%
6. Commerce	-15.7%
7. Education	-13.5%
8. Veterans Affairs	+5.9%
9. Homeland Security	+6.8%
10. Defense	+10%

Source: Office of Management and Budget

Congress writes the budget, not the president, but the document known as the "skinny budget" is what presidents use to signal their priorities. And those priorities, translated into dollars and cents, would deal a blow across the Golden State, which receives $105 billion in federal funding each year—from biomedical research to projects aimed at cleaning up the state's air and water. ▼

The state's large defense industry would reap a windfall, as a result of Trump's proposed $54 billion hike in military spending.

There's also more money for deferred maintenance at Yosemite and other national parks, though less money for park-related construction. Forest Service wild land firefighting also gets a boost.

For every California winner, there's a loser in the 50-plus budget blueprint, making parts of the broad proposal unpalatable for Golden State lawmakers, including some Republicans. Its long-term congressional political prospects are uncertain, at best.

The state's prisons and county jails would no longer be reimbursed for incarcerating undocumented immigrants, a potential loss of more than $50 million for California alone. The community block grants that have ranged in recent years from $4.2 million for Sacramento and $6.2 million for Fresno to $541,000 for Turlock would disappear.

The budget blueprint proposed by President Donald Trump would mark an abrupt federal withdrawal from the artistic and environmental projects that Californians hold dear, slashing wetlands restoration and zeroing out the funding of nearly 20 federal agencies—from the Corporation for Public Broadcasting, a major funding source for NPR and PBS stations, to the national endowments for the arts and humanities.

The spending plan would boost defense spending by $52.3 billion, while eviscerating the Environmental Protection Agency's $8.2 billion budget by a staggering 31 percent, which could slow clean-up of California's hundred-plus Superfund sites, and the State Department's by nearly 29 percent.

The proposed increase in military spending would come at the expense of federal funding for a wide range of projects, including cancer research at UC San Francisco, BART and Caltrans improvements, and the restoration of the East Bay's Dotson Marsh to a wetland habitat.

By contrast, California's defense contractors and military installations could be in for a windfall if President Trump persuades Congress to boost Department of Defense (DoD) spending by 10 percent.

Nearly $50 billion in defense spending already flows to California each year, more than any other state besides Virginia, according to the National Conference of State Legislators.

The DoD contributes billions of dollars each year to state economies through the operation of military installations.

This spending helps sustain local communities by creating employment opportunities across a wide range of sectors, both directly and indirectly. Active duty and civilian employees spend their military wages on goods and services produced locally, while pensions and other benefits provide retirees and dependents a reliable source of income. States and communities also benefit from defense contracts with private companies for equipment, supplies, construction, and various services such as health care and information technology.

According to an analysis by the DoD Office of Economic Adjustment (OEA), the department spent $408 billion on payroll and contracts in Fiscal Year 2015, approximately 2.3 percent of U.S. gross domestic product (GDP). Spending was highest in Virginia, followed by California, Texas, Maryland and Florida. Virginia has the largest defense spending as a share of state GDP at 11.8 percent, followed by Hawaii at 9.9 percent.

B. CALIFORNIA'S PART IN THE U.S. CONGRESS

The **U.S. CONGRESS** *is made up of two U.S. Senators from California and 53 California members to the U.S. House of Representatives.* California has the largest contingent to the Congress. California's ability to influence national legislation is high, but their ability to organize as a pro-California coalition is another question. The 2017 number of Democratic and Republican representatives is 39 Democrats (74%) and 14 Republicans (26%).

C. FEDERAL AND CALIFORNIA LEGISLATURES

Because of the possible confusion between the legislative houses of the United States and California, a U.S. Senator will always have the "U.S." in front of the word "Senator" and a "state senator" will be referred to as such. Similarly, a member of the U.S. House of Representatives must be distinguished from the state assembly to the California legislature in Sacramento. For a complete breakdown of the State legislature, see Chapter 7.

D. U.S. SENATE (U.S. Senators)

A *U.S. SENATOR is one of two representatives from each state who together form the upper chamber of the federal legislature consisting of 100 members.* California can elect only two members to the U.S. Senate. Each U.S. Senator must be at least 30 years of age and have been a U.S. citizen for nine years. A U.S. Senator serves a six-year term. The two U.S. Senators from California may represent the largest concentration of citizens in the U.S., but each have only two votes. U.S. Senators are elected from the entire state. A candidate for the U.S. Senate must spend a large amount of time and money campaigning throughout the state.

California has two female U.S. Senators—the long-time senior Senator, Diane Feinstein, and our junior Senator, Kamala Harris.

An *INCUMBENT is the person currently occupying a specific elective office.* Our federal system greatly favors the incumbent U.S. Senate and the current U.S. House of Representatives member, because of their name recognition and an already established campaign organization.

Senator Diane Feinstein's term expires in 2018. Ms. Feinstein would be 92 at the end of her fifth term if she were re-elected. Speculations about possible replacements include 28th District Congressman Adam Schiff, whose media profile increased through his position as the ranking Democratic member on the House Permanent Select Committee on Intelligence.

E. U.S. HOUSE OF REPRESENTATIVES

U.S. CONGRESSIONAL MEMBER is the term used to address a member of the U.S. House of Representatives. There are currently 53 Congressional members of the House of Representatives elected from California (the number of representatives is based on population). Although they receive the same salary as a U.S. Senator ($174,000), they do not enjoy the same recognition due to the fact that there are only two of the latter.

www.house.gov (House of Representatives)
www.senate.gov (Senate)
www.whitehouse.gov (President)

IV. State and Federal Reapportionment

A. REDISTRICTING MEANS POLITICAL POWER

Redistricting takes place each decade after the U.S. Census is completed. The information gathered from the 2010 census will not be updated until the 2020 census. *REDISTRICTING (reapportionment) is the process by which California's Citizens Redistricting Commission redraws the district lines for California's members of the U.S. House of Representatives, and at the same time, redraws district lines for its own state legislature.*

B. REDISTRICTING: POWERFUL LEGISLATIVE TOOL

The political party that controls the state legislature has the "assured power" in California to decide how state legislative districts and federal congressional districts are to be drawn. The legislature is obligated to divide these districts in a way that serves the interests of the citizens living there.

The Democratic party completely controls both the California Senate and the California Assembly. This is called a SUPERMAJORITY.

The U.S. Presidency and U.S. Congress are controlled by Republicans. With California having a Democrat-controlled supermajority, there is bound to be some head butting between the two.

V. Comparing the California and Federal Governments

A. GENERAL POWERS OF THE U.S. GOVERNMENT

As a republic, the "ultimate power" within the American system rests with the people.

The federal government, under the powers of the U.S. Constitution, is given the power to make laws, veto laws, oversee foreign policy and national defense, impose tariffs, impeach officials, enter into treaties, interpret the Constitution, interpret laws and revise laws that allow one state to impede on the rights of another. The U.S. Constitution has the Bill of Rights, which are the first ten amendments. The *BILL OF RIGHTS guarantees personal liberties and limits the powers of government.*

The U.S. Constitutional protections generally apply to state law by means of the Fourteenth Amendment. As such, **California government and its Constitution are prohibited from violating fundamental rights provided by the United States Constitution**.

The 10th amendment also gives power to the states to govern themselves.

Although the U.S. Constitution outlines general guidelines for issues that fall under state versus federal rule, there are areas of ambiguity that have sparked controversial power struggles. Since its inception, however, there have been many circumstances where it's unclear which government should have the final say. **One of the functions of the U.S. Supreme Court is to interpret state versus federal power**, but even the laws that grant the U.S. Supreme Court its power lack the clarity to avoid accusations of abuse of power. The United States, by design, is a nation of "united" states, meaning that the power of the federal government was intended to be limited.

President Trump professes to believe in the sanctity of state rights.

Working closely with the states, the federal government creates certain laws and programs that are federally funded, but administered by the states. Education, social welfare, assisted housing and nutrition, homeland security, transportation, and emergency response are key areas where states deliver services using federal funds and subject to federal guidelines. In this way, the federal government gives itself power to influence each state.

One of the most hotly contested issues in politics, however, is "big government versus state government" and which entity should have more power.

B. MAIN FUNCTIONS OF OUR CALIFORNIA LEGISLATURE

STATE LEGISLATURES make the laws that govern the states. Unlike the U.S. Congress, which **deals with issues like foreign policy and national security**, our legislature handles many of the issues that affect constituents in their day-to-day lives: **marriage and family law, wills and estates, penal law and state infrastructure**. Our legislature establishes the *STATE BUDGET; the way in which the government allocates taxes and spending of money during a fiscal year* (see Chapter 10). This creates a layer of overlap with the federal government because **our legislature decides how to fund federal programs**.

Our legislature checks its governor in much the same way the U.S. Congress checks the president. It can override vetoes, impeach (recall) government officials, and amend the state constitution. California's governor has the additional power to "blue line" (cut) any item in the budget that he or she feels is too costly through the **Line-Item Veto** process, whereas the U.S. President does not posses such power.

Our legislature also possesses the important but complicated **power of enabling amendments** to the U.S. Constitution. According to Article V of the Constitution, the California legislature can apply to Congress for a national convention to propose constitutional amendments and then ratify the proposed amendments.

C. THE CALIFORNIA CONSTITUTION COMPARED TO THE U.S. CONSTITUTION - BRANCHES OF GOVERNMENT

1. The Legislative Branch

Both California and federal constitutions create and use a *BICAMERAL LEGISLATURE, which consists of two legislative houses.* The California legislature is comprised of the State Assembly (an 80 member body) and the State Senate (a 40 member body).

In both the Assembly and Senate of the California legislature, representation is based on defined districts that are determined by the size of the population. By contrast, the federal legislature has a bicameral legislature in which representation is based on the core democratic principle of one person, one vote in the U.S. House of Representatives (53 members—based on state population) and a U.S. Senate where all states, big and small, are represented by two senators.

State Senators are elected for four years in California whereas U.S. Senators serve six year terms. In both the State Assembly and U.S. House of Representatives, terms are for two years.

All state legislators in California are limited to serving two terms.

2. The Executive Branch

The chief executive in both the federal and state governments (President and Governor) are quite similar. The differences are in the other parts of the executive branch (see Chapter 6).

In the state of California, the Lieutenant Governor (the equivalent to the U.S. Vice President) is elected by the voters and runs separately from the Governor.

The Attorney General, Controller (Chief Financial Officer, parallel to the Secretary of the Treasury), Secretary of State (enforces the state's election laws), Superintendent of Public Instruction, Insurance Commissioner, and the Treasurer are all elected by the voters, whereas these same or parallel functions at the federal level are appointed by the President as part of the **Executive Cabinet** (see Chapter 6).

3. The Judicial Branch

In the judicial branch, we also see a greater degree of voters having direct control in the state government than at the federal level.

The California Constitution states: "Judges of the California Supreme Court shall be elected at large and judges of the state Courts of Appeal shall be elected in their districts at general elections at the same time and places as the Governor. Their Terms are twelve years..." (Article VI, Section 16A). This is after the justices are appointed by the Governor and confirmed by the Commission on Judicial Appointments (see Chapter 8).

California Superior Court justices who are appointed by the governor to fill out emergency vacancies must run for the balance of their terms at the next regularly scheduled general election.

This clearly contrasts with the appointment of federal judges by the President (subject to the consent of the U.S. Senate), whose powers at that level are further enhanced by the fact that **justices in all federal courts serve life terms**.

4. Additional Comparisons

There is a system of **checks and balances** (veto, override) between the three branches of government. Both federal and state constitutions include a Bill of Rights.

As a state, California has specific constitutional guidelines for such fundamental state responsibilities as provisions for local governments within the state, like education, transportation marriage, energy, and water. The state constitution has greater detail on managing such matters, whereas the federal constitution is a general framework for

Presidential Executive Orders
(How many students will be affected if there are changes in Covered California health plans?)

A *PRESIDENTIAL EXECUTIVE ORDER (EO) is a directive issued to federal agencies, department heads, or other federal employees by the President of the United States under his new statutory or constitutional powers.*

Article II, section 1 of the U.S. Constitution reads, in part, "The executive power shall be vested in a president of the United States of America." And, Article II, section 3 asserts that "The President shall take care that the laws be faithfully executed..."

Since the Constitution does not specifically define executive power, critics of executive orders argue that these two passages do not imply constitutional authority. But, Presidents since George Washington have argued that they do and have used them accordingly.

The original purpose of executive orders was to simply establish details of legislation already passed by the President and Congress.

Executive orders are controversial because they bypass Congress. How will California be affected under Trump's leadership?

New incoming presidents may choose to retain the executive orders issued by their predecessors, replace them with new ones of their own, or revoke the old ones completely.

The president can amend or retract his or her own executive order at any time.

President Trump promised to repeal many of President Obama's executive orders—including many aspects of Obamacare and environmental regulations.

operating the federal government. **In general, the state's constitution is much longer and more complex.** California added direct democracy, which added the initiative, referendum, and recall to its constitution during the era of progressive reforms at the turn of the 20th Century (see Chapter 4).

California's former Governor Hiram Johnson is considered the "Father of Direct Democracy" as he helped institute the recall, referendum, and initiative.

Even without the initiative process, California courts have interpreted the state Constitution as providing greater protections for certain rights than the federal Constitution. For example, the federal Constitution may not protect owners against unintended physical damage to private property, even where the government is clearly responsible. **By contrast, California courts recognize that the state and its municipalities may incur liability for reasonably foreseeable damages caused to private property during the course of public works projects, even if the damages were unintended.**

VI. Chapter Summary

The Native Americans, or Indians, were California's first inhabitants. They numbered around 150,000 before the Europeans arrived to "settle" the region. By 1900 there were only around 16,000 Indians left.

The Spanish arrived next. **Juan Rodriquez Cabrillo** sailed up the west coast and was the first European visitor to California (1542). **Father Junipero Serra** established a chain of missions starting in 1769. Each mission was a day's horseback ride from the next. **Presidios** (frontier forts) were established to protect the missions. **Pueblos** (small settlements) also sprang up at places like San Jose and Los Angeles.

In 1821, Mexico broke from Spain. Huge land grants in California parceled grazing land into **ranchos**. California broke from Mexico and became a U.S. possession under the **Treaty of Guadalupe Hidalgo** in 1847. The next year, gold was discovered at Sutter's Mill in the Sacramento area. Gold fever resulted in a massive population growth that has hardly slowed since the time of the "forty-niners." Statehood followed on September 9, 1850, when the state constitution was approved and California joined the union as the **31st state**.

Railroads were the dominant force in the new state's economic growth for fifty years. The **"Big Four"** of the Central Pacific Railroad (Stanford, Huntington, Hopkins, and Crocker) wielded unquestionable political and economic power. The construction of the **transcontinental railroad** brought thousands of Chinese to California to work under near-slavery conditions. Changes in the California constitution were framed to restrict Chinese labor but they also brought into effect some of the great progressive elements of our state system: free public schools, the eight-hour workday, laws governing monopolies and corporations, and the tools of direct democracy: **recall, referendum**, and **initiative**. The **Progressive Party** under **Governor Hiram Johnson** furthered this progressive movement with more constitutional reforms in 1911.

Police powers, the right to protect the public health, safety, morals and welfare, are held by the state while certain concurrent powers, such as taxing and borrowing money, are shared with the federal government. California has two seats in the **United States Senate** and 53 congressional seats in the **United States House of Representatives**. We have more representatives in Congress than any other state. And with each new census, we can expect that number to continue to increase.

The U.S. Presidency and U.S. Congress are controlled by Republicans whereas California has a Democratic **supermajority**. The **14th Amendment** prohibits states from violating our U.S. Constitutional Rights. The **10th Amendment** gives power to the states to govern themselves.

The U.S. Congress deals with issues like **foreign policy** and **national security**, and state legislatures deal with everyday issues like **marriage** and **family law**, among others.

There is an overlap between the federal government and our state legislature when it comes to budget, because our legislature determines how to fund federal programs. President Trump has threatened to withhold federal funds if California does not go along with his new federal policies, such as immigration and deportation enforcement.

VII. Class Discussion Questions

1. What were the contributing factors that lead to the demise of the California Native Americans?

2. What was the "function" of the mission system in California?

3. What political issues did the second California State Constitution in 1879 change?

4. Explain what powers the 10th amendment to the constitution of the United States gives the state of California.

5. What is redistricting, and whom does it protect?

Chapter 3

Voters, Primaries, and General Elections

www.sos.ca.gov (Secretary of State)
www.calvoter.org (Nonpartisan)
www.smartvoter.org (League/Women Voters)

I. Voting Guidelines

A. WHO MAY VOTE?

You are eligible to register to vote in California if you meet the following criteria:

1. You are 18 years old or older on election day.

2. You are a U.S. Citizen.

3. You are a resident of California.

4. You haven't been found mentally incompetent by a court.

5. The voting rights of those incarcerated have changed. See the folowing pages.

Elections and Voter Information - Secretary of State's website
http://www.sos.ca.gov/elections

B. REGISTER TO VOTE (We All Encourage This)

In order to vote you must be a registered voter. A *REGISTERED VOTER is an eligible voter who has filled out an affidavit of registration and delivered it to the county clerk's office or registrar of voters at least 15 days before an election.*

Chapter Outline

The Secretary of State oversees the voting process, but the actual administering of the voting is a county and city function.

1. Online Voter Registration

To register to vote you must complete a brief voter registration application on paper or online. When you **register online** (http://registertovote.ca.gov), the system will search the Department of Motor Vehicles (DMV) database for your California driver license or identification card number, date of birth, and last four digits of your social security number. If your information is found and you authorize elections officials' use of your DMV signature, an electronic image of your DMV signature will be added to your voter registration

AB 2466 - Voting Rights Clarification Becomes Law
Felons in County Jails Can Vote!

Despite widespread opposition from law enforcement (including the California State Sheriffs' Association and the California Police Chiefs Association), Governor Jerry Brown signed AB 2466, the "Voting Rights Clarification" bill, into law. The new law will  allow thousands of felons in county jails to vote in California elections as part of an effort to speed their transition back into society.

Why Let Felons Vote?

Supporters believe allowing felons to vote will help speed their transition back into society. Will republicans say this is just another way that democrats are attempting to increase the voter rolls?

Whether this will actually make a difference is yet to be seen—if there is a way to gauge it at all.

Who Supports the Law?

Cosponsors included the ACLU of California, All of Us or None, Asian Americans Advancing Justice California, League of Women Voters of California, Legal Services for Prisoners with Children, Lawyers' Committee for Civil Rights of the San Francisco Bay Area, Mexican American Legal Defense, and Education Fund.

application after you click "submit" at the end of the online application. If there is no signature on file with DMV, all of your information will be transmitted to your county elections office; you will just need to click "print," sign the paper application, and mail it.

An iPad, tablet, or smartphone can be used to fill out California's online voter registration application.

Your county elections official will contact you when your voter registration application is approved or when more information is needed to confirm your eligibility.

2. Submit or Pick Up a Voter Registration Form

You may submit your voter registration application through the Secretary of State's website. You can also pick up an application

at your county elections office, any Department of Motor Vehicles office, and many post offices, public libraries, and government offices. To have a paper application mailed to you, call your **county elections office** or the Secretary of State's toll-free voter hotline at (800) 345-VOTE.

Official Voter Information Guide - Secretary of State
http://voterguide.sos.ca.gov/

If you are enrolled in California's Confidential Address Program, Safe At Home, please do not attempt to register to vote using this site. For information on how to register to vote, contact the Safe At Home program toll free at (877) 322-5227.

3. Voter Registration Applications in Other Languages

The California Secretary of State's online application is available in **English, Spanish, Chinese, Hindi, Japanese, Khmer, Korean, Tagalog, Thai, and Vietnamese.**

4. Name or Party Changes and Other Information

The registration of a voter is permanent, unless canceled by the registrar of voters. If you move into a new precinct, change your name, or change your political party, you should correct this information with your county registrar of voters as soon as possible. All of the information on your **voter registration form is public information** that can be obtained by anyone for his or her own personal use.

If you have legally changed your name, you should **re-register** to vote so that your voter record reflects your current name. The California Secretary of State recommends that you update your DMV record as soon as you change your legal name.

http://registertovote.ca.gov

5. Confidential Parts of Voter Registration Information

The voter registration rolls are not available to the general public. However, California law allows certain voter information to be released to a member of the California Legislature or U.S. Congress, or to any candidate, any committee for or against a proposed ballot measure,

The "Motor Voter" Act

The "Motor Voter Act" is intended to streamline the process of signing up to vote and encourage more participation in elections  It was put in place in 2016, but the DMV said in a statement that it would not send information to the secretary of state until that office "develops regulations, completes a statewide database system and funding is secured to implement this program." Secretary of State Alex Padilla stated that he expected the process to be in effect no later than the next election cycle.

What is the process?

When people go to the DMV to obtain or renew a driver's license, or to get a state identification card, they'll be asked for the usual information in such transactions, such as their name, date of birth, and address. They'll also be asked to affirm their eligibility to vote and **will be given the choice of opting out of registering at that time**. Information about anyone who does not decline registration will be electronically transmitted from the DMV to the secretary of state's office, **where citizenship will be verified and names will be added to the voter rolls.**

This is not really "automatic" registration—no one who is eligible will be registered to vote without their knowledge.

What about people in the country illegally who obtained drivers' licenses in California?

Padilla noted that there is already a separate process for residents in the country illegally to apply for **special licenses**. Although citizens are currently offered the opportunity to register to vote at the DMV under an earlier federal law, **non-citizens are not**. That will continue under the new registration process.

"We've built the protocols and the firewalls to not register people that aren't eligible," Padilla said. "We're going to keep those firewalls in place."

any person for election, scholarly, journalistic, or political purpose, or for governmental purposes. In these cases, a few items remain confidential and are never provided to any requestor: your social security number, your driver license number, and your signature.

6. Voting By Mail (Absentee)

Any registered voter, including military and overseas personnel, may vote using a vote-by-mail ballot instead of going to the polls on Election Day.

Any registered voter may apply for a "vote-by-mail" ballot by:

1. Completing the vote-by-mail ballot application that is included in your sample ballot, which your county elections official will mail to you prior to each election; or

2. Downloading and completing a **California Vote-By-Mail Ballot Application** from the Secretary of State website; or

3. Contacting your county elections official to see if your county allows you to apply by telephone.

More citizens are voting by mail in all types of elections than ever before.

The application form required to receive a vote-by-mail ballot must be received by your county elections office **no later than seven days before the election**.

For security reasons, California law prohibits casting a ballot over the Internet.

All valid vote-by-mail ballots are counted in every election in California, regardless of the outcome or closeness of any race.

Once your application is processed by your county elections official, your ballot will be sent to you. After you have voted, insert your ballot in the envelope provided, making sure you complete all required information on the envelope. You may return your voted vote-by-mail ballot by:

1. mailing it to your county elections official;

2. returning it in person to a polling place or the elections office in your county on Election Day; or

Same Day - Register and Vote

VoteCal replaced CalVoter and provides a single, uniform, centralized voter registration database that meets applicable **Help America Vote Act (HAVA)** requirements. VoteCal has become the official repository for the voter registration data (the system of record); however, counties will still provide updates and maintenance of the voter registration list by utilizing their existing Elections Management System (EMS), which will be connected to VoteCal.

VoteCal's many functions improve service to the voters of California by:

1. Connecting the Secretary of State and all 58 county elections offices together to improve the voter registration process.

2. Providing a publicly available website which will allow voters to register online.

3. Providing a single, official statewide database of voter registration information.

Voters will be able to access certain public portions of VoteCal to:

1. Apply to register to vote or update their voter registration record.

2. Find their polling place.

3. See if their vote-by-mail or provisional ballot was counted by their county elections official and, if it wasn't, the reason why it wasn't.

Same-day registration will be allowed in local elections now and in statewide elections by 2018.

VoteCal Project
www.sos.ca.gov/elections/voter-registration/votecal-project/

Social Media is Impacting Elections

According to Borrell Associates, political advertising is forecast to continue increasing much more than the last comparable Presidential Election years.

If these figures are true, politicians will have allocated over 9 percent of media budget towards digital and social media—this comes to over $1 billion.

While a large majority of Americans use social media, virtually all of 18-34 years olds use it. 98% admit to using a social platform at least once a month.

Pew Research Center stated that millennials (born 1982-1998) have surpassed baby boomers (born 1946-1964) as the nation's largest living generation, according to population estimates released by the U.S. Census Bureau.

Electoral candidates and their social media agencies are concentrating their efforts towards winning affection of the millennials and finding viable ways to encourage millennials to vote.

President Trump is the King of Twitter.

Not only are candidates utilizing social media, but websites like Facebook, Google, Instagram, Twitter, and Snapchat are also climbing on the bandwagon.

The big question is: who is using social media most effectively? Authenticity is a big thing in social media. Successful candidates are the ones who are the most comfortable using these apps.

But can social media really help change people's minds on politics? We've seen over and over that viewing an image can change the world. Social media generally tends to be very insular. Voters will go online to meet other like-minded people and express their views, which are often, but not always, too entrenched to be swayed by a single Twitter or Facebook post.

The candidates who can take advantage of social media and get their message in front of this new generation may be the most successful in attaining whatever office they seek.

3. authorizing a relative or person living in the same household as you to return the ballot on your behalf. Regardless of how the ballot is returned, it MUST be received by the county elections office by the time polls close at 8:00 p.m. on Election Day. Late-arriving vote-by-mail ballots will not be counted.

II. Primary Elections
(3 Primaries on 1 Ballot)

In California the primary ballot election is made up of three different elections, all on the same ballot. See **Figure 3-1** for a breakdown of three primary elections on one ballot.

The *PRIMARY ELECTION includes the following:*

1. *A top two candidates open primary that selects partisan (political party) candidates for statewide offices;*

2. *A nonpartisan primary that selects county and judicial officials, county party officials, and the State Superintendent of Public Instruction; and*

3. *A presidential primary that selects state delegates, from each political party, to its national nominating convention for president and vice president.*

A. CALIFORNIA USES A TOP TWO CANDIDATES OPEN PRIMARY

California has its primary election on the first Tuesday after the first Monday in June of even-numbered years. It is top two candidates open primary (see Figure 3-1).

Most of the offices that were previously known as "partisan" are now known as "voter-nominated" offices. Voter-nominated offices are state constitutional offices, state legislative offices, and U.S. congressional offices. The only "partisan (party) offices" now are the offices of U.S. President and county central committee.

1. Closed Primary System vs. Modified Closed Primary System

In a *CLOSED PRIMARY SYSTEM, only voters registered in a political party could vote that party's primary Presidential ballot. A "closed" primary system governed California's Presidential primary elections in the past.*

61

Figure 3-1 ## Top Two Candidates Open Primary: How It Works

California voters approved Proposition 14, which created a "top two" open primary election system.

The **TOP TWO CANDIDATES OPEN PRIMARY** applies to most of the offices that were previously known as "partisan (party)" and are now known as "voter-nominated" offices. In California these offices include the following state constitutional offices, legislature, and federal congressman and senators:

1. United States Senators
2. Congressional Representatives
3. State Senators
4. Assembly Members
5. Governor
6. Lt. Governor
7. State Treasurer
8. Secretary of State
9. State Attorney General

Regardless of their party, top two vote-getters go to primary.

Under this system, all candidates running for one of the statewide and congressional offices are listed on one ballot, regardless of their party preference, and all voters will see the same list of candidates, regardless their own party registration.

In a Top Two Candidates Open Primary, **the purpose is simply to reduce the number of all candidates down to two, not to select each party's nominee**. The party preference information on the ballot for each candidate is for informational purposes only. It is possible that two candidates from the same party will go to the general election, if they are the top two vote-getters.

The top two vote-getters for each office will advance to the general election, regardless their party preference. It doesn't matter if one candidate receives a majority of the votes cast: the top two vote-getters always advance to the general election.

Write-in candidates for "voter-nominated" offices can still run in the primary election. However, a write-in candidate can only advance to the general election if the candidate is one of the top two vote-getters in the primary.

The Top Two Primary does NOT apply to elections for: President and Vice President, or Political Party County Central Committees or County Councils. These offices are called "party nominated" offices. Therefore, only candidates running for State Superintendent of Public Instruction or candidates for voter-nominated offices in special elections can win outright by getting a majority of the vote in the primary election.

Presidential Primary - How It Works

If you are registered to vote with a political party, you will be given a ballot for that party in a presidential primary election.

Each political party has the option of allowing people who register to vote without stating a political party preference ("no party preference" voters—formerly known as "decline-to-state" voters) to vote in their presidential primary election. A political party must notify the Secretary of State's office whether or not they will allow no party preference voters to vote in their presidential primary election 135 days before the election.

If a no party preference voter wishes to vote in the presidential primary election of a political party who has notified the Secretary of State that they will allow no party preference voters to vote in their party's primary, a no party preference voter would simply ask his or her county election's office or ask a poll worker at his or her polling place for a ballot for that political party. A voter may not request more than one party's ballot.

If a no party preference voter does not request such a ballot, he or she will be given a nonpartisan ballot, containing only the names of candidates for voter-nominated offices and local nonpartisan offices and measures to be voted upon at that presidential primary election.

Nonpartisan Primary (Election at Primaries)

What is a nonpartisan office?

It is an office for which candidates' names appear on the ballot without political party designation. No party may nominate a candidate for nonpartisan office at the primary election. ▼

Which offices are nonpartisan (no stated political party)?

Local offices such as most city council members, county supervisors, all school boards, all judgeships, including the statewide office or a member of the California Supreme Court. The statewide offices of Superintendent of Public Instruction and Insurance Commissioner are nonpartisan.

Are there nonpartisan primaries?

Yes. Some local nonpartisan primaries, such as those for judges, are usually held at the same time as the statewide regular primary. A candidate for a nonpartisan office who is on the primary ballot is selected if he or she wins more than 50% of the vote. If not, there is a runoff election in November between the top two candidates.

Do all nonpartisan offices use primaries?

No, some nonpartisan offices, such as most city councils and school boards, do not use primaries. Candidates run as independents and

LWV®
LEAGUE OF
WOMEN VOTERS

the person with the most votes wins even if it is not a majority.

Nonpartisan primary information source: League of Women Voters of California®

California uses a "modified" closed primary system for Presidential elections. In a **MODIFIED CLOSED PRIMARY SYSTEM**, *voters who decline to register with any political party are permitted to vote for a party's candidates in a primary election if authorized by that party's rules and duly noticed by the Secretary of State.*

B. THE PRESIDENTIAL PRIMARY

The **PRESIDENTIAL PRIMARY** *is the direct election of delegates to the national party conventions that select nominees for the offices of president and vice president of the United States.* The presidential primary is combined with the regular California primary that is held on the first Tuesday after the first Monday in June of each presidential election year (any year evenly divisible by the number four). The delegates selected go to the national party convention, which is usually held in July or August.

Remember, under the Top Two Candidates Open Primary Act (refer back to Figure 3-1), all candidates running in a primary election, regardless of their party preference, will appear on a single Primary Election ballot and voters can vote for any candidate. The top two overall vote-getters— not the top vote-getter from each qualified party and anyone using the independent nomination process—will move on to the general election.

C. NONPARTISAN OFFICES IN THE PRIMARY

A *NONPARTISAN PRIMARY is a primary election to nominate a candidate for which no political party may legally nominate a candidate, such as judges, school boards, county and municipal offices, and the State Superintendent of Public Instruction.* The election of supreme court judges and appellate court judges is handled differently (see Chapter 8 on Courts). A person who wishes to seek the nomination for a nonpartisan office simply declares his or her candidacy and gathers the signatures required to get on the ballot.

A nonpartisan primary election differs greatly from a partisan primary election in one important aspect: A nonpartisan primary candidate who receives a majority vote in a primary election wins the office instantly without the need of going on to a general election. A *MAJORITY VOTE means that more than fifty percent of the votes cast support one candidate.* If no candidate receives a majority vote in the primary, a run-off election between the two individuals with the largest number of votes takes place in the upcoming general election.

III. General Election

The *GENERAL ELECTION is the election held throughout the nation on the first Tuesday after the first Monday of November in even-numbered years.* Court decisions and federal laws have made voter qualifications and election days uniform across the country. **More people vote in general elections because of the national media visibility of the candidates**.

The big distinction is that, in a primary election, the nominee wins only the right to advance, whereas in the "general election," he or she wins the office.

A. WHO ARE THE LIKELY VOTERS IN CALIFORNIA?

Exit polls have shown over and over that the largest segment of the population that votes has many things in common. Here is what the typical voters in California have in common:

1. Over 60% are Caucasian,
2. Most are homeowners, not renters,
3. Californians 55 and older constitute **45% of likely voters**, and
4. Approximately 41% are college graduates and 41% have some college education.

A high percentage of the younger adults and minorities do not register to vote, or vote as regularly as the older, white population. But it is only a matter of time until Asians, Hispanics, and younger people wake up and join the political process. This group of non-voters is like a sleeping giant just waiting for someone to wake it up and make it aware of its political power.

Bottom line, your vote counts!

After Trump was elected President, many minorities and young people started protesting in the streets. However, that level of passion might be better spent in the voting booth. (Note that California historically is a democratic state, so Hillary Clinton was the clear winner here.)

Regularly Scheduled Election Dates for Each Year

1. Local (Municipal) Election Dates

   April (2nd Tuesday of even-numbered years) or **March** (1st Tuesday, after the 1st Monday of odd-numbered years)

2. Statewide Election Dates

   June (1st Tuesday, after the 1st Monday each year)

   November (1st Tuesday, after the 1st Monday each year)

Elections held in June and November of each even-numbered year are considered California's statewide election dates.

IV. Special Elections

A *SPECIAL ELECTION is usually called by the governor to fill unexpired terms and to decide certain ballot measures.* If there is a vacancy in a U.S. congressional or state legislative office, the governor must call for a special election. When a vacancy occurs in a U.S. Senate or U.S. House of Representative's position after the close of the nomination period in the final year of the congressional term, **the governor may, at his or her discretion, decline to call a special election and appoint a replacement.**

A. ELECTIONS ARE CONSOLIDATED

CONSOLIDATED ELECTIONS mean that the elections for different levels of government are put together on the same ballot on the same election date in order to save money and effort. For example, the presidential primary, on the federal level, is consolidated with the statewide, direct, and nonpartisan primary. This happens only once every four years.

V. Precincts and Ballots

A. PRECINCTS AND POLLING PLACES

The county registrar of voters divides the county into voting precincts. A *PRECINCT is a geographical area made up of a group of voters from a low of 60 to a high of approximately 600, depending on the election and how the registrar of voters wants the voters grouped.*

Each precinct has a precinct board. The board is made up of one inspector, two judges, and three clerks. Each board member must be a voter from that precinct or from a precinct in that area. Any voter may apply to be one of these precinct workers, who usually volunteer for the position. You, as students, can gain important political insight from being a precinct volunteer during a long election day. The *POLLING PLACE (POLL) is the location within a precinct where the voting takes place.* Schools and public buildings are popular polling places because these types of structures are available free of charge. A polling place can be just about anywhere, except a bar or liquor store.

B. ELECTION DAY

On election day, the polls open at 7am. and close at 8pm. This makes for a 13-hour voting period.

C. ABSENTEE BALLOT

An *ABSENTEE BALLOT is a ballot that is sent to you before the election, if you choose not to vote in person at the polling place on election day.* **It must be received back before the close of the polls**. You must apply in writing in order to receive an absentee ballot. Any registered voter may apply for permanent absentee voter status. If you are a permanent absentee voter, you will automatically receive an absentee ballot for each election.

How the Election Recount System Works

An **ELECTION RECOUNT** is a repeat tabulation of votes cast in an election that is used to determine the correctness of an initial count.

Recounts will often take place in the event that the initial vote tally during an election is extremely close.

In the event more than one voter requests a recount of the same office or measure, and at least one request is for a manual recount, the elections official of a county subject to multiple requests shall conduct only one manual recount of those ballots, the result of which shall be controlling.

Recount costs vary by county. Before the recount can begin, the voter or campaign committee represented by the voter requesting the recount must provide the money requested by the county elections official to pay for the cost of the first day's recount work. This procedure is repeated for each day the recount continues.

A recount does not preclude the Secretary of State from certifying the election results. The law requires the Secretary of State to do so no later than 38 days after the election.

All of the ballots cast in the entire state must be recounted in order to change the result in a statewide contest.

If the office, slate of presidential electors, or measure is voted on statewide, unless each vote cast for the office, slate, or measure is recounted, the results of any recount will be declared null and void.

Recount laws and cost vary from state to state.

The absentee ballot has become very popular in recent years. In many campaigns part of the campaign strategy is to send absentee ballot request forms to anyone who supports a particular candidate, whether it is requested or not.

D. CALIFORNIA DOES NOT PURGE

A **VOTER PURGE** is *when the registrar of voters goes through the list of registered voters on a systematic basis and eliminates certain voters from the list.* The usual reason is that the voter has not voted in the last general election. In California there is no annual purge of the voter registration roster. Usually voters who have moved or passed away remain on the voter rolls.

This is why both President Trump and Senator Bernie Sanders implied that the California presidential election may have been rigged.

E. CALIFORNIA'S BALLOT FORMS

California uses a long ballot form. A *LONG BALLOT is a complete list of the offices, items, and propositions to be decided upon by the voters.* We have eleven state executives to elect other than the governor, as well as judges, county officials, and city officials, plus ballot propositions, bond issues, and maybe a charter amendment or two. We may complain about the length of the ballot, but we are reluctant to give up the privilege of deciding many issues ourselves.

California uses the office-block type of ballot. An *OFFICE-BLOCK BALLOT presents all the competing candidates, by office, throughout the ballot.* The voter makes his or her choice in an office-by-office manner. In contrast, some other states use a *PARTY-COLUMN BALLOT, which lists the candidates party-by-party.* At the top of a party column ballot is a box where a single mark will cast a vote for all of the party candidates. In California, however, it is difficult to vote a party ticket. The office-block ballot forces voters to think of candidates as individuals rather than as part of a partisan ballot ticket.

The Electoral College System and How it Works
(Only for President and Vice President Candidates)

The **ELECTORAL COLLEGE** *is made up of 538 electors who cast votes to decide the President and Vice-President of the United States.*

When voters go to the polls in a presidential election they will be deciding which candidate receives their state's electors. Currently, a majority of 270 electoral votes is required to elect the President.

Your state's entitled allotment of electors equals the number of members in its Congressional delegation: one for each member in the House of Representatives plus two for your Senators.

The Electoral College is a *process*, not a place. The founding fathers established it in the Constitution as a compromise between election of the President by a vote in Congress and election of the President by a popular vote of qualified citizens.

The Electoral College process consists of the selection of the electors, the meeting of the electors where they vote for President and Vice President, and the counting of the electoral votes by Congress.

Under the 23rd Amendment of the Constitution, the District of Columbia is allocated three electors and treated like a state for purposes of the Electoral College.

Each candidate running for President in your state has his or her own group of electors. The electors are generally chosen by the candidate's political party, but state laws vary on how the electors are selected and what their responsibilities are.

The presidential election is held every four years on the Tuesday after the first Monday in November. You help choose your state's electors when you vote for President because when you vote for your candidate you are actually voting for your "candidate's electors."

Most states have a "winner-take-all" system that awards all electors to the winning presidential candidate. However, Maine and Nebraska each have a variation of "proportional representation."

The meeting of the electors takes place on the **first Monday after the second Wednesday in December after the presidential election**. The electors meet in their respective states, where they cast their votes for President and Vice President on separate ballots. Your state's electors' votes are recorded on a "Certificate of Vote," which is prepared at the meeting by the electors. Your state's **Certificates of Votes** are sent to the Congress and the National Archives as part of the official records of the presidential election.

Each state's electoral votes are counted in a joint session of Congress on the **6th of January** in the year following the meeting of the electors. Members of the House and Senate meet in the House chamber to conduct the official tally of electoral votes.

The Vice President, as President of the Senate, presides over the count and announces the results of the vote. The President of the Senate then declares which persons, if any, have been elected President and Vice President of the United States.

The President-Elect takes the oath of office and is sworn in as President of the United States on January 20th in the year following the presidential election.

In the 2016 Presidential election, Donald Trump received 304 electoral votes to Hillary Clinton's 227. Seven "faithless" electors voted for other candidates, costing Trump two votes and Clinton four. Hawaii's votes—three for Clinton and one breaking from the state's results and supporting Bernie Sanders-were the last to be counted.

2016 Electoral College Results

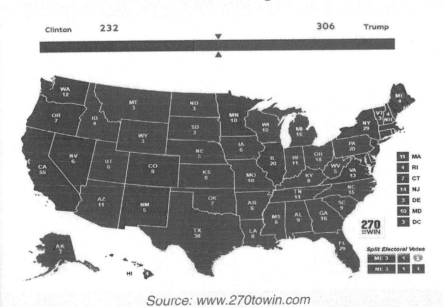

Source: www.270towin.com

VI. Chapter Summary

A person in California may fill out an affidavit of registration and register to vote (at least **15 days before an election**) if he/she is 18 years old, a U.S. Citizen, and a resident of California.

Online registration is available through **http://registertovote.ca.gov** (the Secretary of State's website) and the Department of Motor Vehicles. Once approved, your county election's official will contact you and voter packets may be picked up at various government offices.

Any registered voter may vote by mail instead of going to a polling place on election day.

California uses a **modified closed primary system** for presidential elections. The California Primary Election includes: a **top two candidates primary** for statewide offices, a **nonpartisan primary** to select county and judicial officials, county party officials, and the State Superintendent of Public Instruction, and a **presidential primary** to select state delegates from each political party to nation conventions to nominate president and vice president of the United States.

The **Top Two Candidates Open Primary Act** states that all candidates running in a primary election, regardless of their party preference, appear on a **single primary election ballot**, enabling voters to vote for any candidate. The top two vote-getters move on to the general election. The **general election** is held throughout the nation on the first Tuesday after the first Monday of November in even-numbered years.

Likely voters in California are over 60% white, and mostly homeowners. Persons over 55 years old make up 45% of likely voters and approximately 41% are college graduates, with 41% having at least some college education.

A **special election** is usually called by the governor to fill unexpired terms of U.S. Congressional or state legislative offices, and to decide certain ballot measures.

Elections are **consolidated** in order to facilitate the election process at the various local, state, and national levels.

The County Registrar of Voters divides the county into **voting precincts** that represent geographic groups of voters. Each precinct has a precinct board made up of registered voters from that precinct, consisting of a one inspector, two judges, and three clerks. The **polling place** is the place within the precinct where the voting takes place, which can be schools or public buildings or any other convenient location.

On **election day** the polls open at 7am and close at 8pm.

For persons choosing not to vote at a polling location, an **absentee ballot** may be used, but must be received back before close of polls on election day.

California uses a **long ballot** form, which is a complete list of the offices, items, and propositions to be decided upon by the voters. California uses the **office block ballot** to present all the candidates by office throughout the ballot, which enables the voters to think of candidates as individuals instead of part of a partisan ticket.

VII. Class Discussion Questions

1. How is a modified closed primary different from a blanket primary?
2. What is the presidential primary?
3. Who is most likely to vote in California?
4. Discuss the three main types of ballots.

Chapter 4

Direct Democracy

https://ballotpedia.org/History_of_Initiative_and_Referendum_in_California

In 1911, amendments to the state constitution gave us the three basic tools of direct democracy:

I. THE RECALL

II. THE REFERENDUM

III. THE DIRECT INITIATIVE

These three political tools removed some of the partisan politics from government and gave California voters the right to help set public policy. These reforms are still with us today.

The Father of California Direct Democracy

Governor Hiram Johnson, "The Progressive Reformer," Republican Governor – 1911-1917 (two terms).

Hiram Johnson, the "Progressive" Republican, was overwhelmingly voted into the governor's office because he, as did a majority of voters, disliked the political power of the railroad monopoly that had been building for decades. His goal was to "kick the Southern Pacific Railroad out of politics." A large number of Progressive Republicans and Democrats joined together to support the progressive idea and cause. ▼

Chapter Outline

Hiram Johnson on the campaign trail

A **PROGRESSIVE** *in those days was usually thought of as favoring the restriction of corporate influence in politics and expanding the citizens' participation in politics, while protecting the environment and improving working and living conditions.*

The Progressive reformers saw political parties as the instrument that the Central Pacific Railroad (later acquired by lease from the Southern Pacific Railroad) monopoly had used to dominate the state government for over four decades.

The Progressives' main objective was to weaken the political party system in California, dominated by the Southern Pacific Railroad. These reforms are still with us today.

Hiram Johnson's Progressive Reforms That Changed California

1909 REFORMS

The direct primary law was enacted. Candidates for public office must be nominated at a special election called a direct primary, not at a party convention, which had been the practice. This eliminated the "behind closed door" selection of party candidates.

1911 REFORMS

The Railroad Commission, which regulated the railroads and all the utilities, was increased from three to five members who were now appointed by the governor instead of being elected.

The direct democracy initiative, referendum, and recall, became part of the state constitution. Now the voters could actually reverse or make laws themselves, or vote an official out of office.

Judicial and school board elections became nonpartisan.

Women obtained the right to vote. The U.S. Constitution was not amended to include women's suffrage until 1920.

Office-Block Ballot was introduced. Voters vote for each office separately.

1913 REFORMS

City, county, and local special district elections became nonpartisan.

The leadership and operation of political parties was defined in detail by law.

Cross-filing was permitted by candidates, allowing them to run for the same office or each party in the primary election. Cross-filing was abolished by Governor Earl Warren.

Hiram Johnson is called the "Father of California Democracy."

Three Tools of Direct Democracy
I. The Recall

The **RECALL** *is a procedure whereby any California state elected official can be removed from public office, before the completion of his or her term.* It has been a fundamental part of our governmental system since 1911 and has been used by voters to express their dissatisfaction with their elected representatives. **Any elected (state-level) official may be recalled (removed from office) for any reason, but the procedure does take time and effort**.

The citizens of California are granted the authority to perform a recall election by Article 2, Sections 13-19 of the California Constitution.

The authority to conduct a recall election in California applies to officials at the state and local levels. These include the elected offices of Governor, Lieutenant Governor, Secretary of State, Treasurer, Controller, Attorney General, Superintendent of Public Instruction, Insurance Commissioner, Members of the State Board of Equalization, State Legislators, and Justices of Courts of Appeal and the State Supreme Court. A state officer appointed in lieu of election or to fill a vacancy in one of these offices may also be recalled.

The State Constitution requires that the legislature must provide for the recall of "local officers." This provision, however, does not affect counties and cities whose charters provide for recall.

As with most states, the right of recall in California does not extend to recalling federal politicians, California's two U.S. Senators and fifty-three members of the U.S. House of Representatives, because they hold federal offices, which have different removal procedures.

A. PREPARING THE NOTICE OF INTENTION TO RECALL (State Officer)

To begin recall proceedings against a state officer, the recall proponents **must serve, file, and publish or post a notice of intention to circulate a recall petition**.

The proponents should ensure that the notice of intention complies with California law. If a notice of intention is found to be deficient, the proponents will be required to prepare a new notice of intention, including the collection of signatures. The notice of intention must contain:

1. The **name and title of the officer** sought to be recalled.

2. A statement, not over two hundred words in length, of **the reasons for the recall**. A reason must be provided, but under Article II, Section 14(a) of the California Constitution, the sufficiency of this reason is not reviewable.

3. **The printed name, signature, and residence address of each proponent of the recall**. If a proponent cannot receive mail at his or her residence address, the notice of intention must also contain a mailing address for the proponent. The number of proponents that sign the notice of intention must be at least 10 or equal to the number of signatures required to be filed on the nomination paper of the officer sought to be recalled, whichever is greater.

4. **The text of Elections Code section 11023**, which describes how the officer sought to be recalled may file an answer.

B. SERVE AND FILE THE NOTICE OF INTENTION

A copy of the notice of intention must be **served by personal delivery or by certified mail on the officer sought to be recalled**. In addition, the original of the notice of intention, along with an affidavit of the time and manner of service, must be filed with the Secretary of State within seven days of being served.

C. PUBLISH THE NOTICE OF INTENTION

A copy of the notice of intention (including addresses and signatures) **must be published at the proponents' expense at least once in a newspaper of general circulation**. The publication need not include the text of Elections Code section 11023. If there is no newspaper of general circulation in the jurisdiction of the officer whose recall is being sought, the proponents may satisfy the publication requirement by posting the notice of intention in at least three public places within the jurisdiction.

D. OBTAIN AND FILE PROOF OF PUBLICATION

The proponents **must file proof of publication** at the same time that they file two blank copies of the proposed recall petition with the Secretary of State. Proof of publication is obtained from the newspaper publisher after the notice of intention appears in print.

E. ANSWER OF RECALLEE

Within seven days after the filing of the notice of intention, **the officer sought to be recalled may file with the Secretary of State an answer** of not more than two hundred words.

The answer must be signed and accompanied by the printed name, and business or residence address of the officer sought to be recalled.

If an answer is filed, the officer must, within seven days after the filing of the notice of intention, serve a copy of the answer, by personal delivery or by certified mail, on one of the proponents named in the notice.

F. PREPARE THE RECALL PETITION

The next step in the recall process for state officials requires the proponents to **prepare the recall petition for circulation**. The Secretary of State is required to provide a format for the petition (see **Figure 4-1**), and may also be obtained from any county elections official. The recall petition format prepared by the Secretary of State is mandatory and must be used.

All petition sections must be printed in uniform size and darkness with uniform spacing.

Noncomplying petition forms will be rejected as invalid.

G. RECEIVE APPROVAL OF THE RECALL PETITION

Proponents must file two blank copies of the proposed petition with the Secretary of State within ten days after the filing of the answer to the notice of intention, or, if no answer is filed, within ten days after the expiration of the seven-day period for filing the answer. The Secretary of State must, within ten days of receiving the copies of the petition, determine whether the proposed form and wording of the petition meet the necessary requirements and notify proponents in writing of the findings. If it is found that the petition does not meet the requirements, the notification must include a statement of what alterations in the petition are necessary. Then, the proponents must file two blank copies of the corrected petition with the Secretary of State within ten days after receiving the notification.

The submitted blank copies of the petition will be carefully reviewed for uniformity correctness and will be compared to the notice of intention and publication to assure accuracy in text, punctuation, capitalization, spelling, format, etc. If the comparison discloses discrepancies, the petition will be rejected.

Figure 4-1

PETITION FOR RECALL

TO THE HONORABLE _____(See note[1])_____

Pursuant to the California Constitution and California election laws, we the undersigned registered and qualified electors of the _____(See note[2])_____ of _____(See note[3])_____, California, respectfully state that we seek the recall and removal of _____(See note[4])_____, holding the office of _____(See note[5])_____, in _____(See note[2])_____, California.

We demand an election of a successor to that office. (See note[6])

The following Notice of Intention to Circulate Recall Petition was served on _____(Date)_____ to _____(See note[4])_____:

(Insert complete text of Notice of Intention here)

The answer of the officer sought to be recalled is as follows:

(Insert Officer's Statement here—200 words or less)
(If no statement, insert "No Answer was Filed")

Each of the undersigned states for himself/herself that he or she is a registered and qualified elector of the _____(See note[2])_____ of _____(See note[3])_____, California.

Column must be at least 1" wide

	PRINT YOUR NAME	RESIDENCE ADDRESS ONLY		
	1. _____			
	YOUR SIGNATURE AS REGISTERED TO VOTE	CITY	ZIP	
	PRINT YOUR NAME	RESIDENCE ADDRESS ONLY		
	2. _____			
	YOUR SIGNATURE AS REGISTERED TO VOTE	CITY	ZIP	
	PRINT YOUR NAME	RESIDENCE ADDRESS ONLY		
	3. _____			
	YOUR SIGNATURE AS REGISTERED TO VOTE	CITY	ZIP	

DECLARATION OF PERSON CIRCULATING SECTION OF RECALL PETITION
(MUST BE IN CIRCULATOR'S OWN HANDWRITING)

I, _____(See note[7])_____, solemnly swear (or affirm) all of the following:

1. That I am 18 years of age or older.
2. That my residence address, including street and number, is _____.
   (If no street or number exists, a designation of my residence adequate to readily ascertain its location is _____.)
3. That the signatures on this section of the petition form were obtained between _____(Month and Day)_____, 20_____, and _____(Month and Day)_____, 20_____; that I circulated the petition and I witnessed the signatures on this section of the petition form being written; and that, to the best of my information and belief, each signature is the genuine signature of the person whose name it purports to be.

I certify under penalty of perjury under the laws of the State of California that the foregoing is true and correct.

Executed on _____(Date)_____ at _____(City or Community Where Signed)_____, California.[8]

_____   _____
Circulator's Signature   Date

[1] Insert here – Secretary of State of California if for a state officer, or name of the appropriate governing body if local. The authority which orders or "calls" elections for that office, or the governing authority for that jurisdiction should be named.

[2] Insert Electoral Jurisdiction here – County, City, District name, as appropriate.

[3] Insert geographical location here – City, County, etc., as appropriate.

[4] Insert here – name of person whose recall is being sought.

[5] Insert here – name of office.

[6] In case of Supreme Court or Appellate Court Justice, request shall be that the Governor appoint a successor.

[7] Insert here – Printed full name of person who gathered signatures.

[8] The petition must be set in at least 8 point type. If signature spaces are printed on both sides of a sheet of paper, the above information, except for the declaration of circulator must appear on each side of the paper. The circulator's declaration must follow the last signature box. It is suggested that petition be printed on 8 ½" x 14" paper in order to maximize the number of signatures spaces printed on a sheet of paper.

SOS 05/16/14

The ten-day correction notification period and ten-day filing period for corrected petitions is repeated until the Secretary of State finds that no alterations are required.

No signatures may be obtained on the recall petition until the form of the petition has been approved by the Secretary of State.

H. NUMBER OF SIGNATURES REQUIRED

For a statewide officeholder, the recall petition must contain signatures equal to **12% of the votes cast in the last election**. Signatures must be obtained from at least five different counties and must be equal in number to at least one percent (1%) of the last vote for the office in each of five counties. For the recall of local officials, the recall petition must contain from **10% to 30%**, depending on the number of registered voters in the electoral jurisdiction. Within **160 days** from the time the Secretary of State notifies the proponents that the form and wording of the petition is correct, proponents must file a petition with the requisite number of valid signatures.

Governor Gray Davis Recalled

Possibly the most famous recall election in history took place in California in October 2003, when Governor Gray Davis was recalled and Arnold Schwarzenegger took his place. Two years of a continuing budget crisis prompted Congressional Representative Darrell Issa to fund a "Petition" to recall Governor Gray Davis. The general public faulted Governor Davis and the Legislature for mismanaging the energy crisis, overspending during the stock market bubble, and the resulting tax increases, including a 300% increase in auto registration fees (taxes).

Over 134 candidates qualified for the recall ballot process by paying the $3,500 filing fee, obtaining 10,000 signatures, or by a combination of the two.

Do not confuse recall with impeachment. Recall is initiated by the voters for any reason. *IMPEACHMENT is conducted by the state legislature to remove an official from office for a serious violation of the law.*

II. Referendum
(Some Laws Need Voter Approval)

A referendum requires the voters at a general election to either suspend "existing laws" or approve only certain taxes, constitutional amendments, or bonds.

A. REFERENDUM BY PETITION

A **REFERENDUM (BY PETITION)** *is the process of approving or rejecting statutes or parts of statutes passed by the legislature (with the approval of the governor over his or her veto) until it can be voted on by the electorate.*

The referendum by petition, which suspends a statute before becoming law, requires the signatures of at least five percent of registered voters who cast votes for governor in the last election. The Secretary of State certifies that the petition has the required number of signatures and is submitted on time (within 90 days after enactment of the bill at a regular session and 91 days after a special session).

Once petitions are filed, county elections officials have eight working days to determine a raw count of the signatures submitted and report their findings to the Secretary of State.

If the referendum petition qualifies, the law is not enforceable until after the next election, where the voters have a chance to formally accept or reject the new law.

B. COMPULSORY REFERENDUM

Do not confuse the referendum by petition with the compulsory referendum. The **COMPULSORY REFERENDUM** *automatically requires voters at an election to approve a legislature-approved constitutional amendment, charter, or bond issue before it can become law.*

The amount of votes required for passage of a compulsory referendum vary depending on the nature of the referendum.

1. Increase Property Taxes for Infrastructure Bonds and School Facility Bonds

Generally speaking, property tax increases for infrastructure bonds require approval by two-thirds of the local voters. Property tax increases for school facility bonds that satisfy certain conditions, however, require approval by 55 percent of local voters.

2. General Taxes

A general tax requires approval of a simple majority of voters. A *GENERAL TAX is a tax: 1) levied by a general purpose government—city or county—and 2) expended, at the discretion of the local government's governing body, on any programs or services. A SIMPLE MAJORITY is 50 percent of voters plus one additional voter.*

3. Special Taxes

Special taxes require approval from two-thirds of local voters. A special tax is a tax that meets one of the folowing conditions:

 a. **Special Purpose District Tax.** All taxes—other than property taxes for infrastructure bonds—levied by special districts, school districts, and community college districts are special taxes.

 b. **Tax Dedicated to a Specific Purpose.** A city or county tax dedicated to a specific purpose or specific purposes—including a tax for specific purpose deposited to the agency's general fund—is a special tax. All non-property taxes that cities and counties are authorized to levy may be raised as special taxes.

 c. **Tax Levied on Property**. All taxes levied on property other than the property tax—typically parcel taxes—are special taxes.

Referendum and the following initiative measures only appear on general election ballots.

III. Direct Initiative
(The People Can Put an Issue to a Vote)

In 1911, an amendment to the California Constitution established the California initiative process, giving voters the right to enact legislation.

The people of California have another wonderful power; they can make laws without the help of the legislature or the governor through a process known as the direct initiative. A *DIRECT INITIATIVE is a process by which the people draft a proposal or constitutional amendment and acquire enough voter signatures to place the issue on the ballot, where it can be decided by all California voters.* **If a majority of the voters approve the measure, it becomes law**. The direct initiative can be on any topic, but must be limited to a "single subject." The governor has no veto power over a direct initiative.

The legislature's only role in the direct initiative is to hold a legislative committee hearing 30 days prior to the election.

A. INITIATIVES ARE POPULAR

The longer 150-day qualification period is the key to why so many initiatives are put before the voters. If a trade group, association, or some other type of interest group has the desire, it can usually put an initiative before the people by hiring professionals to circulate the initiative petitions. Today, one can hire a company just to gather initiative signatures. They usually charge the initiative sponsors from 80 cents to $1.25 for each signature.

B. INITIATIVE REFORM

The rejection by voters of numerous initiatives in general elections has opened the door to possible changes in California's initiative process. The question is: are we really ready to change our initiative system?

California voters may not be as dumb as some professional signature-gathering firms think. Have some self-generating initiative organizations gone too far by cranking out too many new initiative campaigns? Interest groups that saw the initiative process fail to get their legislation passed by the voters are instead looking to lobbying the legislature as an answer.

C. PROPOSITIONS

The three types of propositions are referendum, compulsory referendum, and direct initiative.

The Secretary of State gives an initiative or a referendum a proposition number when it meets the necessary qualification requirements for the ballot. A *PROPOSITION (Prop.) is a qualified ballot measure that is given a number from one of these three sources: (1) referendum petition – prevents laws from going into effect; (2) compulsory referendums – legislatively-approved constitutional amendments and bond issues, which must always be approved by the voters; and (3) direct initiatives – people-approved petitions that can put any issue on the ballot for voter approval.* To avoid confusion with past and current ballot measures, a law was passed to consecutively number propositions starting with the 2002 general election and running in twenty-year cycles. The next cycle will start in 2022.

D. SAMPLE: PROPOSITION 54 (<u>Referendum</u>)
The Legislature Transparency Act

Most politicians like the ability to make last-minute backroom deals and insert them into "surprise" legislation, bypassing controversy or to pass bills that may not hold up to public scrutiny.

That's a good reason why lawmakers have resisted years of attempts by good-government advocates to end the practice known as "gut and amend."

In a move that would have made Hiram Johnson proud, in 2016 the voters of California passed Proposition 54—**The Legislature Transparency Act. It ended what many considered the state legislature's unethical practice of removing the text of bills at the last moment and replacing it with unrelated legislation that is quickly put up for a vote—with no chance for the public to view, comment, and act on it**.

The proposition is intended to ensure the proceedings of both houses of the legislature and their committee hearings be video recorded and posted on the Internet.

The legislation:

1. Prohibits legislature from passing any bill unless it has been in print and published on the Internet for at least 72 hours before the vote, except in cases of public emergency.

2. Requires the legislature to make audiovisual recordings of all its proceedings, except closed session proceedings, and post them on the Internet.

3. Authorizes any person to record legislative proceedings by audio or video means, except closed session proceedings.

4. Allows recordings of legislative proceedings to be used for any legitimate purpose, without payment of any fee to the State.

Like most good things, this transparency will come with a cost—$1 million a year. But is it really that much in a multi-billion-dollar budget? How expensive is it when compared to the money at stake when special interests get their favorable proposals into last-minute legislation that the public never sees?

Enacting this reform did what the legislature itself refused to address. This was the optimal use of a ballot proposition.

E. VOTER PAMPHLETS

A *VOTER BALLOT PAMPHLET* is a booklet sent before the election to each voter explaining propositions and ballot measures. Different positions and issues on the statewide ballot are presented by the Secretary of State while the city and county clerks help clarify local ballot measures. The Secretary of State states:

> "Many rights and responsibilities go along with citizenship. Voting is one of the most important, as it is the foundation on which our democratic system is built. Read carefully all of the measures and all related information contained in this pamphlet. Referendums, legislative propositions, and citizen-sponsored initiatives are designed specifically to give us, the electorate, the opportunity to influence the laws which regulate us all." See the L.A. City and County information pamphlets on the following page.

The biggest complaints refer to the initiative qualification requirements. Grassroots groups with little money to spend can't get their propositions to the voter.

Other critics want more disclosure of the interests and political forces supporting or opposing initiatives. Some want to simplify the ballot so that the average voter can read the initiative once and understand it.

F. ARE PROPOSITIONS GOOD OR BAD?

The basic good thing about propositions is that they allow the voters to vote directly for a proposed law.

The bad thing about propositions is that lobbyists with unlimited funds can flood the airways with ads and the streets with people to collect signatures on petitions. A great deal of the time, these ads or signature collectors do not fully explain what the proposition is all about.

Sometimes there are so many propositions on the ballot that voters simply do not have the time to read through the pages of information.

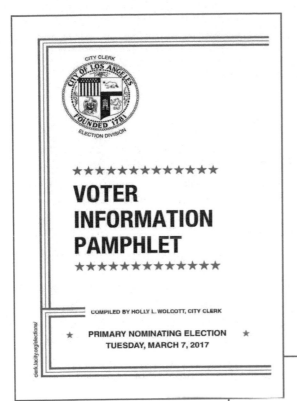

★★★★★★★★★★★★★

VOTER
INFORMATION
PAMPHLET

★★★★★★★★★★★★★

COMPILED BY HOLLY L. WOLCOTT, CITY CLERK

★ **PRIMARY NOMINATING ELECTION** ★
TUESDAY, MARCH 7, 2017

072

Dean C. Logan
Los Angeles County
Registrar-Recorder/County Clerk

Official Sample Ballot
Consolidated Municipal and Special Elections
March 7, 2017

Polls open at 7 am and close at 8 pm

lavote.net

IV. Chapter Summary

During the "Progressive" era when Hiram Johnson was governor of California (1911-1917), sweeping reforms were made in the state election laws, empowering voters with a more direct form of democracy than was previously enjoyed. The **direct primary** was created, allowing voters from each party to choose their party candidates for major state offices, rather than relying on the traditional party convention. Certain local, judicial, and school board seats became nonpartisan. Women received the **right to vote in California** (although the federal government didn't catch up until 1920). The office-block ballot was introduced, requiring voters to vote for each office separately, rather than voting for an entire party slate with a single stroke. But the most important progressive reform of this period was the creation of the recall, referendum, and initiative.

The **recall** is a procedure by which a state official may be removed from office by a vote of the people. This is not **impeachment,** where an officeholder is removed for a violation of the law. A recall may be (and in 2003 was) based only on public dissatisfaction. A recall petition is circulated and must be signed by a percentage of the voters (this number varies depending on the office). After a maximum period of 160 days of circulation, if the petition has the proper number of signatures, the governor must call for a recall election. The public is asked to vote "yes" or "no" to the recall and to choose a replacement from a list of candidates. The replacement with the most votes will finish out the term. If the public votes "no" to the recall, the officeholder is safe for at least six months, then a new recall can be initiated. In local elections there is no successor section on the recall ballot. The successor is either appointed by the city council or the office remains vacant until the next election.

The recall election on October 7, 2003 stunned the nation and put Arnold Schwarzenegger in the governor's office. He has since been replaced by Governor Jerry Brown for two terms.

A **referendum** allows the public to block an unwanted law from taking effect. A **petition** (signed by at least five percent of the registered voters who cast votes for governor in the previous election) must be presented to the Secretary of State within 90 days of the enactment of the bill, making it unenforceable until after the next election, where the voters may formally reject or accept it.

The **direct initiative** process allows voters to enact laws for themselves. An initiative is a proposed law or state constitutional amendment initiated by the people. A petition with the proper number of signatures will place an initiative on the ballot for the people to decide in the next election. Initiatives and referendums appear on the ballot as Propositions with a number assigned to each by the Secretary of State.

Remember, only California state and local officials can be recalled. Federal officials cannot be recalled.

V. Class Discussion Questions

1. Why is Hiram Johnson referred to as the father of direct democracy in California?

2. What group benefits the most from the recall, the initiative, and the referendum?

3. Can you think of an instance when the recall may be a bad idea and not in the best interest of democracy?

4. Have the people in California come to rely too heavily on the initiative process?

5. Why do you think there is a 150-day limit to gather signatures for an initiative or referendum?

Chapter 5

Interest Groups, Political Parties, and Campaigns

I. Interest Groups

We have a large state that is very diverse. It is an amazing society of varying interests and ideas. But all interest groups have one thing in common: they want California's elected officials to know how they feel about their pet issues. It is the stated purpose of interest groups to influence people in such a way that interest groups' points of view will be accepted.

The largest interest groups are: unions, corporations, and professional associations.

An **INTEREST GROUP** *is an organized group having a common interest that attempts to persuade others to see its point of view.* Its objective is to have public policy makers embrace its goals and ideas. For example, the California Association of REALTORS® is made up of over 120,000 real estate brokers and salespeople who foster the concept of home ownership—the "American Dream"—and work to protect their sale's commissions.

Small groups can have much more of a political impact on legislation if they join forces. The League of California Cities, for example, maintains offices, libraries, researchers, and several lobbyists at a fraction of what the cost would be if each city tried to represent its own interest. Almost every city in the state is a member.

A. DIFFERENT TYPES OF INTEREST GROUPS

Interest groups differ greatly as to money, size, and goals. **PRIVATE AGENDAS** *are specific objectives set by an interest group in order to help it accomplish a specific goal.* These groups are as diverse as the California Trial Lawyers Association and the Sierra Club.

Chapter Outline

The **United Farm Workers of America (UFW)** is the largest farm worker union in the country. Larry Itliong, the Filipino leader of the Agricultural Workers Organizing Committee, began a strike against the Central Valley grape growers in the 1960s and, instead of crossing picket lines as in the past, Cesar Chavez, the head of the National Farm Workers Association  (made up almost exclusively of Mexicans), joined the Filipinos and created the UFW. In addition to bettering the working conditions of the union members, the UFW has become so powerful that **in 2017 the courts upheld that migrant farmworkers had the right to be paid overtime for their labor.** This groundbreaking decision would not have been imaginable just a few decades ago.

TRUMP ANXIETY

President Trump showed that Twitter and other social media sites are very effective in delivering messages instantaneously to his 28 million social media followers. Twitter circumvents the role of political parties costly advertising.

More importantly, President Trump spent far less money on Twitter and social media than his political opponents did on mainstream news outlets. Social media is the modern form of communication. It is credited with winning the White House.

Corporate leaders get anxious when President Trump turns his Twitter account on them to compel corporations to reduce government costs. As an example, when the cost of Boeing's Air Force One "ballooned" and the President tweeted Boeing leaders about it, Boeing's shares fell.

Public employee unions have grown to the point that they control the powerful votes of teachers, city employees, firemen, and the staff of most hospitals.

B. BUSINESS GROUPS

Most large corporations and trade associations have representatives in Sacramento. Apple, Facebook, Google, Chevron, and other California-based firms protect their interests by having lobbyists in the state capital. *TRADE ASSOCIATIONS are organizations made up of similar businesses whose goal is to promote their common interests.* Their goal is straightforward; they want to stay in business by continuing to provide goods or services to the consumer, and, at the same time, make a profit. The California Chamber of Commerce represents many different types of firms, but other trade associations represent specific types of businesses, like the California Manufacturer's Association or the California Retailer's Association.

Unions, Corporations, and Professional Associations

1. BUSINESS

California Chamber of Commerce, California Manufacturers Association, California Bankers Association, California Retailers Association, California Association of REALTORS®

2. AGRICULTURE

California Farm Bureau Federation, Agricultural Council of California, United Farm Workers

3. LABOR (UNIONS)

California State Employees Association, California Teamsters Public Affairs Council, California Labor Federation

4. PROFESSIONAL ASSOCIATIONS

California Medical Association, State Bar of California

5. EDUCATION

Association of California School Administrators, California School Boards Association, California Teachers Association, California Federation of Teachers

6. GOVERNMENT

County Supervisors Association, League of California Cities

7. IDEOLOGICAL ORGANIZATIONS

American Civil Liberties Union (ACLU)

8. RACIAL, ETHNIC, OR RELIGIOUS ORGANIZATIONS

National Association for the Advancement of Colored People (NAACP), Mexican-American Political Association (MAPA), California Catholic Conference

9. PUBLIC UTILITIES

Pacific Gas & Electric, Department of Water and Power

10. MISCELLANEOUS

League of Women Voters, California Taxpayers Association, Sierra Club, Girl Scouts, Boy Scouts, American Association of Retired Persons (AARP)

Public Employee Unions Create Special Budget Problems!

52.9% of California government workers are in Public Employee Unions, while only 9.4% of non-government workers are in private unions.

Government Public Employee Unions have created a different set of financial problems for the state, governor, legislature, county supervisors, city councils, Boards of Trustees, and Boards of Education in that their costs are higher than average. By law, the government must bargain in good faith with organized groups of employees, such as public employee unions.

Trade unions negotiating with profit-making corporations have no say in who their bosses will be, as they do not directly elect corporate board members. **Public employee unions, however, essentially elect their bosses**. For example, in the Board of Education elections, the Teachers Union selects potential "pro union" candidates whom they help sponsor and finance, in addition to manning the phones to get out the Election Day vote.

These municipal unions in California have built up a hugely effective political machine with the faces of police officers, firefighters, nurses, and the largest group, teachers, prominently displayed in their ads. It's hard to say "no" to large pay and pension increases to such honorable people, and they deserve fair pay and benefits. However, some people believe the level of influence exercised by their leaders is inappropriate, and economically detrimental to the state, county, or city. Is it too much power without fiscal discipline or accountability?

Thanks to the power wielded by the Public Employees Unions, the state has over-promised retirement benefits. (See Chapter 9 for more details.)

If these **"unfunded liabilities" (debts)** were to be paid, it could very well lead to bankruptcy for the cities and counties, if not the state. Rather than face this overwhelming fiscal crisis, the government unions continue to fight to keep their overly inflated retirement packages using the political power they have in the form of finances and sheer numbers of members.

C. DEMOGRAPHIC INTEREST GROUPS

DEMOGRAPHIC INTEREST GROUPS are groups of people who share characteristics such as income, age and education. The LGBT (Lesbian, Gay, Bi-sexual, Transgender) community is an example of a powerful demographic interest group.

The gay and lesbian rights and issues lobby is composed of organizations that represent the interests of the lesbian, gay, bisexual and transgender population and their supporters. These groups have undertaken a growing civil rights campaign for sexual orientation and gender identity equality and have achieved several milestones in recent years, including the legalization of gay marriage in California, and addressing the continued need for AIDS treatment and research.

Legislators typically respond to the grievances and demands of interest groups. Legislators need the vote and support of these groups because they tend to be the most active and powerful in supporting or undermining their re-election campaigns. Indeed, legislators tend to seek support of the vocal, motivated, active, and highly visible individuals in interest groups when setting out to raise funds and organize their continuing campaign efforts. The LGBT community is just such a group.

D. SINGLE-ISSUE GROUPS

Groups formed to publicize only one particular issue or subject are known as *SINGLE-ISSUE INTEREST GROUPS. The Pro-Choice Movement and Right-to-Life Advocates are two such groups.*

Proposition 64, California's legalization of recreational marijuana, passed in November of 2016, is an example of a single-issue interest group issue (see pages 100-101).

E. LOBBYISTS

Interest groups hire men and women to represent them in our state capital, Sacramento. These people are referred to as lobbyists.

A *LOBBYIST is a person acting for specific interest groups who tries to influence the introduction of legislation and the votes taken on bills in the legislature.* Sometimes lobbyists are referred to as the **"third house of the legislature"** because they have as much influence over legislation as the Assembly and the Senate.

Endorsements and PACs
(Political Action Committees)

An **ENDORSEMENT** *is an official show of support to a candidate from an important source.* Endorsements come from interest groups, celebrities, newspapers, other political leaders, and state or county political committees. Endorsements for nonpartisan races were prohibited in 1986 by a constitutional amendment.

In a campaign, real political muscle comes from the ability of a candidate to obtain crucial endorsements and generate campaign contributions, especially from PACs. **PACs (POLITICAL ACTION COMMITTEES)** *are subgroups within large organizations, such as corporations, trade groups, unions, and grass roots groups that contribute campaign funds to candidates who support their political view.* It is much easier for a candidate to build a campaign "war chest" from PACs because large contributions are granted with little effort, and they may often include a powerful endorsement.

F. WHAT MAKES A SUCCESSFUL LOBBYIST?

Some people may be surprised to find that money, gifts, and expensive meals are not the tools used by a successful lobbyist. Lobbyists are not usually loud, but are pleasant and non-offensive. A good lobbyist uses "the soft sell approach" by convincing the official that it is important for him or her to listen. A smart lobbyist is well organized, direct, and succinct in his or her presentation. The golden rule is never make a legislator look bad or uninformed.

In Sacramento, where most law-making is done by committee, it is best for the lobbyist to schedule, with the legislator's office, a one or two minute walking meeting between committee meetings. This lobbying technique is best described by the term "schmooze." *SCHMOOZE is the term used by lobbyists to describe the art of discussing business in a casual, social manner.*

G. CROWD LOBBYING

CROWD LOBBYING is the practice of mobilizing large numbers of people to attend organized rallies timed to influence a decision or specific legislation. The group, if successful, will draw news media attention and attain free publicity for its cause.

California Legalizes Marijuana Use... What Will This Mean for the California Economy?

In November 2016, California voters passed **Proposition 64**, the **California Marijuana Legalization Initiative**. California joins four states—**Colorado, Washington, Oregon and Alaska**—who previously decriminalized recreational cannabis. Referred to by supporters as the "Adult Use of Marijuana Act (AUMA)," the measure allows adults age 21 and older to possess up to one ounce of marijuana, cultivate up to six plants, and sets rules for commercial cultivation, manufacture, and sale. It includes rules aimed at keeping cannabis products from children, preventing impaired driving, and requiring licenses for sellers.

Before Prop 64, California arrested about 20,000 people a year for marijuana felonies and misdemeanors and has about 10,000 people incarcerated for pot offenses.

Under the new law, those marijuana arrests will stop. Everyone sitting in jail or prison for a marijuana offense may be eligible to apply for release. Similarly, all those people who have had marijuana offenses may be eligible to have their record reclassified.

It will still be possible to be arrested for a marijuana offense in California. Possession of more than an ounce (or more than four grams of concentrate) will be a crime punishable by up to six months in jail. Possession of less than an ounce can be a misdemeanor offense if it is on school grounds during school hours. Similarly, cultivation of more than six plants without being a permitted medical marijuana patient or without a license is still a crime, but typically only a misdemeanor (with some exceptions) punishable by a maximum of six months in jail.

Minors under 18 who get caught with pot are hit with an infraction punishable by drug education, counseling, or community service, but no fines. People between 18 and 21 get an infraction with a maximum

$100 fine. Adults who possess pot on school grounds during school hours get a misdemeanor, however minors under 18 will only be hit with an infraction.

With a population of nearly 40 million people, and a thriving medical marijuana trade legalized 20 years ago, California already has the United States' largest legal marijuana market.

Legalization of recreational pot should generate an estimated $1 billion in additional taxes per year.

The measure designates state agencies to license and regulate the industry and imposes a 15 percent excise tax on retail marijuana sales. There's also a cultivation tax, although it exempts medical pot from some taxation.

Several desert communities in Southern California have opened their arms to large-scale marijuana cultivation businesses as a way to create local jobs and more tax revenue.

Industry experts point out there's been an increase in investor interest and activity to fund indoor and outdoor cultivation, testing laboratories, infused product manufacturers, as well as licensed marijuana shops. According to the Deputy Director of the National Cannabis Industry Association, 115 new California companies have joined since January, 2016, bringing total membership in the state to 330.

Analysts point out the marijuana businesses face added risks due to federal banking laws regarding deposits from the marijuana industry and other challenges unique to the industry.

For example, Section 280E of the U.S. tax code dings businesses engaged in "trafficking in controlled substances" by barring them from getting the deductions or credits available to other businesses.

The Federal Controlled Substances Act considers marijuana a "Schedule I" drug, even though it has been legalized in California. This contradiction continues to be the cause of much debate and confusion.

II. Political Parties

A. CALIFORNIA'S POLITICAL PARTIES

A *POLITICAL PARTY is a large organization of voters who have similar views and band together to gain more power*. Because of our primary elections and the large number of nonpartisan local government positions, the California political party machinery is not as strong as it is in other states.

What's the Story Behind the Political Party Animals?

The **Democratic donkey** was first associated with Democrats in a 1828 presidential campaign. Cartoonist Thomas Nast later used the Democratic donkey in newspaper cartoons and made the symbol famous.

Nast invented another famous symbol—the **Republican elephant**—in a cartoon that appeared in *Harper's Weekly* in 1874.

Democrats today say the donkey is smart and brave, while Republicans say the elephant is strong and dignified.

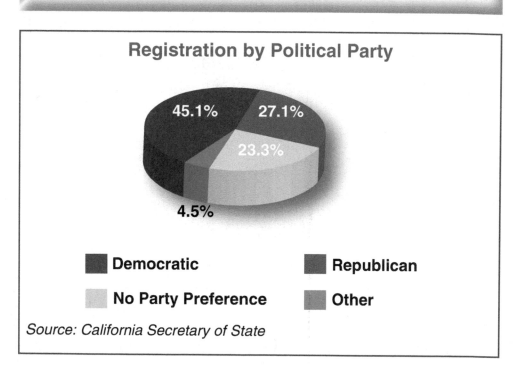

Registration by Political Party

45.1% 27.1%

23.3%

4.5%

■ Democratic ■ Republican

■ No Party Preference ■ Other

Source: California Secretary of State

History of Political Parties in California

Since the statewide party nomination process began in 1910, nineteen parties have qualified to participate in primary elections, including:

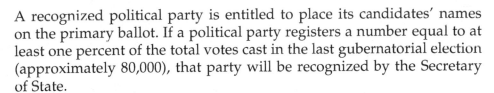

* Democratic 1910-present
* Republican 1910-present
* Independence League 1910
* Prohibition 1910-1962
* Socialist 1910-1938
* Progressive (Bull Moose) 1912-1918
Liberty 1932-1934
Commonwealth 1934-1938
Communist 1934-1944
Progressive 1934-1938
Townsend 1938-1942
Independent Progressive 1948-1954
American Independent 1968-present
Peace and Freedom 1968-1998; 2003-present
Libertarian 1980-present
Green 1992-present
Natural Law 1995-2006
Reform 1995-2002
Americans Elect 2011-2015

* Active before 1910

A recognized political party is entitled to place its candidates' names on the primary ballot. If a political party registers a number equal to at least one percent of the total votes cast in the last gubernatorial election (approximately 80,000), that party will be recognized by the Secretary of State.

More and more voters are switching to "no party preference."

The political parties recognized by the Secretary of State in California are:

American Independent	www.aipca.org
Democratic	www.cadem.org
Green	www.cagreens.org
Libertarian	www.ca.lp.org
Peace and Freedom	www.peaceandfreedom.org
Republican	www.cagop.org

103

After initially being qualified by the secretary of state, an organization must maintain a membership equal to at least two percent of the total votes cast in the last gubernatorial election or lose its legal existence.

B. DEMOCRATS AND REPUBLICANS

Of course, the two major political parties are the Republicans (GOP) and the Democrats (Dems). Most voters in California are either Democrats or Republicans, but it is very common to cross party lines in the privacy of the voting booth. *TICKET-SPLITTING is when a person votes for different political parties, depending on the office.* For example, people may vote for a Republican governor, a Democratic lieutenant governor, a Republican attorney general and a Democratic state treasurer.

It is said that Democratic voters seem to dominate the coastal areas (western sections) of our state, whereas Republicans mainly cluster in the inland eastern parts of California.

C. POLITICAL LABELS

A *CONSERVATIVE is a person or philosophy that tends to favor established traditions, lower taxes, smaller government, and resistance to change.* We often speak of **conservatives as being to the "right"** and **liberals as the "left."** In American politics, conservatives tend to identify with the Republican party, but a person may also be thought of as a conservative Democrat if he or she identifies with the "right" on certain issues.

A *LIBERAL is a person or philosophy that tends to favor political reform or progress, more regulations, a larger government, more taxation, and is open to ideas that challenge established traditions.* Liberals generally lean towards more government spending paid for by increased taxation. In American politics, liberals tend to identify with the Democratic party; however, people might see themselves as liberal or "moderate" Republicans.

Labels such as "conservative" and "liberal" are useful in providing a general idea of where a person stands on certain issues. In reality, however, many individuals will fluctuate greatly between these positions, depending on the issue.

D. STATE CENTRAL COMMITTEE

Each recognized political party has a State Central Committee and a County Central Committee. The *STATE CENTRAL COMMITTEE is made up of partisan office holders, nominees, appointees, and other minor party officials.* It does not represent the rank-and-file party member.

Each party has large state central committees that break down into several parts. The *EXECUTIVE COMMITTEE of each party is a small group of high party officials who meet often to conduct party business in the party name.*

The State Central Committees adopt resolutions, coordinate fund raising, and encourage party enthusiasm. Campaigning is done by each individual candidate's organization and any helpful interest groups. The State Central Committee's effectiveness is minimal because of California's political traditions and our state's large size.

E. COUNTY CENTRAL COMMITTEE

A *COUNTY CENTRAL COMMITTEE is the county political party group elected by popular vote from assembly districts.* Additional members are party nominees from within the district. The Los Angeles area, which forms one of the largest groups, has over three hundred members on the county committee. County party committees have the job of helping candidates with their campaigns, but like the state committees, they have little effect. Besides, a recent statute has prohibited California political parties from endorsing a candidate before the primary election. Our state laws discourage political parties from having a strong and effective state and county representation.

F. POLITICAL REFORM ACT

The *POLITICAL REFORM ACT was instituted to oversee more than 100,000 candidates for state and local government, their campaign funds, and the activities of lobbyists.* This proposition ensures that a state ballot pamphlet will be an independent, useful document sent to each voter, and that laws or practices unfairly favoring incumbents will be abolished. To achieve these goals, the Political Reform Act provides the following:

1. Conflict of interest rules for government officials.
2. Disclosure requirements for candidates, committees, lobbyists, and public officials.
3. Nonpartisan ballot pamphlets that analyze and present the actual text of existing laws and proposed changes.

The *FAIR POLITICAL PRACTICES COMMISSION is a five-member, bipartisan state panel responsible for the administration and enforcement of the Political Reform Act.* The commission may impose direct fines of $2,000, and higher fines through civil suits. All fines are paid into the state treasury, not the agency itself.

G. ELECTION LAWS

Several election laws have established that:

1. Legislators cannot receive any gift over $250.

2. Members of state boards and commissions are now subject to the maximum $250 honorarium and limit on gifts.

3. Legislators are now, for the first time, prohibited from voting on legislation that would be a conflict of interest.

4. Legislators and members of state boards and commissions are prohibited from lobbying the legislature for at least one year after leaving office.

III. Campaigns

A. POLITICAL CAMPAIGNS

Strategy is the key to every well-run political campaign. A *CAMPAIGN STRATEGY is a well-thought-out tactical plan to win an election as its goal. This is accomplished by identifying the audience, the message, the delivery, and timing, while considering the campaign resources.*

The most important element of a good campaign strategy is to develop a good campaign message. The *CAMPAIGN MESSAGE is the theme of the person or the issue that the campaign will attempt to communicate to voters.* The complex issues of a campaign must be reduced down to a simple message that sets the candidate apart from all others.

B. PAST ELECTIONS OFFER VOTER PATTERNS

VOTER TARGETING is the deliberate attempt on the part of a campaign to identify the precincts or election districts in which to consolidate its effort in order to win. Voter targeting uses past voter patterns and turnouts as the best indicator of future voting patterns for the same precinct. Precincts that have not been committed to a particular political party are called swing voters.

The *SWING VOTERS are the individual voters who have not committed themselves to a particular political party, issue, or candidate but, if presented with an appealing campaign message, may vote for that issue or candidate.* These swing voters should be the most targeted because this group may produce the biggest switch to your side with the least campaign cost and effort.

Proposition 56:
$ 2.87 a Pack (California Tobacco Taxes)

Proposition 56 increased the tobacco tax by $2.00, bringing the total tobacco tax up to $2.87 per pack of cigarettes. The tobacco tax was levied on other tobacco products and e-cigarettes as well. Revenue from the additional $2.00 tax was allocated to physician training, prevention, and treatment of dental diseases, Medi-Cal, tobacco-use prevention, research into cancer, heart and lung diseases, and other tobacco-related diseases, and school programs focusing on tobacco-use prevention and reduction.

No on 56 out-raised supporters two-to-one in proposition funding. Yes on 56 had received $35.53 million, while opponents had raised $70.98 million. Two of the largest cigarette manufacturers in the U.S., Philip Morris USA, R.J. Reynolds Tobacco Company, and their affiliates, together contributed over $69 million to No on 56. Supporters' biggest donor was Tom Steyer, who contributed over $11.55 million. The California Democratic Party backed the measure, and the California Republican Party opposed it. It passed, nonetheless.

A *VOTER LIST is the list of registered voters by name, address, party affiliation and, in California, phone number that is supplied for a small charge, precinct by precinct, to the purchaser from the county registrar of voters.* Not only can individuals or campaigns buy voter lists, but they can also buy precinct results of past elections with a list that identifies who voted in that particular election. But relax—they can not tell anyone how a person actually voted!

President Trump has shown us that vast amounts of money spent on an election may be reduced by simply tweeting daily.

IV. Campaign Laws in California

A. CALIFORNIA POLITICAL REFORM ACT

All California candidates and political committees must file a periodic campaign statement listing information regarding financial contributions and expenditures. It is filed with the Fair Political Practices Commission in Sacramento. The report must be signed by the filer, under penalty of perjury, confirming that it is true and correct. All

Fair and Balanced? You Decide!

Over the last decade, unbiased news is harder to obtain. Perhaps the best an informed person can do is to read a variety of different news sources to arrive at a personal opinion.

Reading news on the Internet is becoming more popular, and is beginning to compete with the mainstream media. Newspaper and television audiences and advertising are expected to decrease by about 5% per year over the next decade.

Even old, established nonpartisan organizations, such as the League of Women Voters, appear to many to have become more liberal. With 36 million members, the AARP (American Association of Retired Persons) has been accused of promoting policies favorable to the elderly and financially harmful to young working people. One example is increased Social Security and Medicare paid for by imposing high income and payroll taxes on the working young.

Biased News: **Fox News, RT** (Mostly takes a conservative point of view)

ABC NBC, CBS, CNN, MSNBC (mostly takes a liberal point of view)

Neutral: www.calvoter.org (a nonpartisan organization)

California: www.ss.ca.gov (California Secretary of State)
www.ca.gov (California State)
www.governor.ca.gov (California Governor)

Fake News: Facebook has been "called out" for publishing a tremendous amount of fake news stories. CEO Mark Zuckerberg has promised to address the issue, as billions of its members (especially young people) get their news from social media sites.

advertising must identify the sponsor, and no anonymous contributions over $100 are allowed.

B. LOCAL CAMPAIGN ORDINANCES (Laws)

Local government can adopt its own campaign laws, in addition to the state laws. Some cities and counties have limited corporate contribution amounts and require additional campaign statements.

C. FEDERAL ELECTION CAMPAIGN ACT

The Federal Election Campaign Act applies only to people running for federal office. This law requires candidates to file periodic public reports disclosing financial facts about campaign contributions and expenditures. The law also sets limits on the amount of money that can be contributed by individuals at $1,000 and may go as high as $5,000 for groups. Copies of these reports can be examined at the office of the Federal Election Commission in Washington, D.C.

D. CITIZENS UNITED v. FEDERAL ELECTION COMMISSION

Citizens United v. Federal Election Commission **558 U.S. 310 (2010) is a U.S. constitutional law and corporate law case.**

In the case, the conservative nonprofit organization Citizens United wanted to air a film critical of Hillary Clinton and to advertise the film during television broadcasts shortly before the 2008 Democratic primary election in which Clinton was running for U.S. President. This would violate a federal statute prohibiting certain electioneering communications near an election.

However, the court upheld requirements for public disclosure by sponsors of advertisements. The case did not affect the federal ban on direct contributions from corporations or unions to candidate campaigns or political parties.

The U.S. Supreme Court did something that "changed how money can be spent in elections and by whom."

The Citizens United case gave corporations and unions the green light to spend unlimited sums on ads and other political tools, calling for the election or defeat of individual candidates. An example is the seven and eight-figure donations from people like casino magnate and billionaire Sheldon Adelson who, with his family, has given about $40 million to so-called "super PACs." Contributions to groups that make independent expenditures are unconstitutional.

It is still illegal for companies and labor unions to give money directly to candidates for federal office.

The Supreme Court kept limits on disclosure in place, and super PACs are required to report regularly on who their donors are.

The same can't be said for "social welfare" groups and some other nonprofits, like business leagues. These groups can function the same

way as super PACs, so long as election activity is not their primary activity. But unlike the super PACs, nonprofits do not report who funds them. That's disturbing to those who favor transparency in elections.

V. Chapter Summary

Interest groups consist of people with common goals who organize together in an effort to influence public policy making. These groups come in all sizes and types, organized around many different issues: political, economic, cultural, and social. Small, local groups will often band together on a statewide basis to wield more clout.

Interest groups often engage professional lobbyists to represent them. **Lobbyists** are a big part of the political process in Sacramento, building relationships with lawmakers and persuading lawmakers to support legislation favorable to the groups they represent.

Most politicians align themselves with either of the two major political parties, **Democrats** or **Republicans**. Also recognized in California are the **American Independent**, **Green**, **Peace and Freedom**, and **Libertarian** parties. The **Republican Party** is generally viewed as more conservative than the Democrats, tending to resist radical change in favor of more established traditions and values. The **Democratic Party** is perceived as being more liberal, favoring reform and being more open to new ideas. Each party has its own internal structure including a **Central Committee**, made up of officeholders and party officials throughout the state, and an **Executive Committee** of highly placed party officials who decide policy. Political parties in California don't actually run a candidate's campaign, but they do play a major advisory and organizational role.

A great effort is made to keep elections fair. The **Political Reform Act** places controls on candidates, lobbyists, and campaign funds. This law is enforced by the bipartisan **Fair Political Practices Commission**.

Successful political campaigns are based on careful planning and a sound campaign strategy. The campaign message must often be very simple and straightforward, in order to capture the imagination of the voting public. **Voter targeting** involves identifying key election districts that should be emphasized in campaigning. **Swing voters** are those who might be persuaded either way on an issue, depending on the appeal of the campaign message.

Social media has become an important player in the world of politics—both in fund raising and relaying messages to the masses (particularly young people). President Donald Trump used Twitter to his advantage when campaigning and continues to do so regularly as president.

VI. Class Discussion Questions

1. Is it true that only large business corporations form interest groups?
2. Is it true that interest groups only pull America apart and offer the citizens nothing?
3. Do trade associations only protect the weak?
4. Is it true that the third parties will soon take on the Democrats and the Republicans?
5. Is it true that California has no campaign laws?
6. Do you or your fellow students watch TV news, Internet sources, or social media sites like Facebook for your news?

Chapter 6

The Executive Branch

I. Executive Branch

Jerry Brown, the current *GOVERNOR OF CALIFORNIA, is the chief executive officer of our state government, and because of California's prominence, he is also an influential figure in national politics.* The governor, however, does not act alone. California uses a plural executive system. The California *PLURAL EXECUTIVE system is one that consists of the governor and twelve other elected officials* (see next page). Each of the other eleven members of the plural executive runs a separate part of the state government. This is different from the federal government, where more power is concentrated in the hands of a single chief executive.

TRUMP ANXIETY

The Governor has tremendous power over the state's budget, and with a supermajority of Democrats in the state legislature, he should have no trouble getting much of his agenda financed. However, President Trump and U.S. Attorney General Jeff Sessions (head of the Justice Department that is made up mostly of conservative Republicans), can significantly influence our state's and cities' budgets because we rely heavily on federal block grant funds. Many Californians are anxious that these much needed federal funds will be withheld as a tactic to force us to adhere to policies that do not reflect the will of our liberal state's attitude.

Chapter Outline

After the Governor - Twelve Elected Officials Under the Plural Executive System*

1. Lieutenant Governor - *Gavin Newsom (D)*
2. Attorney General - *Xavier Becerra (D)*
3. State Controller - *Betty Yee (D)*
4. State Treasurer - *John Chiang (D)*
5. Secretary of State - *Alex Padilla (D)*
6. Superintendent of Public Instruction - *Tom Torlakson (D)*
7. Insurance Commissioner - *Dave Jones (D)*
8. State Board of Equalization (Five Members)

Office holders as of this edition publication date

Governors of the State of California
1850-Present

1849-1851: Peter Burnett (Democrat)
1851-1852: John McDougall (Democrat)
1852-1856: John Bigler (Democrat)
1856-1858: J. Neeley Johnson (American)
1858-1860: John Weller (Democrat)
1860-1860: Milton Latham (Democrat)
1860-1862: John Downey (Democrat)
1862-1863: Leland Stanford (Republican)
1863-1867: Frederick Low (Unionist)
1867-1871: Henry Haight (Democrat)
1871-1875: Newton Booth (Republican)
1875: Romualdo Pacheco (Republican, acting)
1875-1880: William Irwin (Democrat)
1880-1883: George Perkins (Republican)
1883-1887: George Stoneman (Democrat)
1887-1887: Washington Bartlett (Democrat)
1887-1891: Robert Waterman (Republican)
1891-1895: Henry Markham (Republican)
1895-1899: James Budd (Democrat)
1899-1903: Henry Gage (Republican)
1903-1907: George Pardee (Republican)
1907-1911: James Gillett (Republican)
1911-1918: Hiram W. Johnson (Republican)
1917-1923: William Stephens (Republican)
1923-1927: Friend Richardson (Republican)
1927-1931: C. C. Young (Republican)
1931-1934: James Rolph (Republican)
1934-1939: Frank Merriam (Republican)
1939-1943: Culburt Olson (Democrat)
1943-1953: Earl Warren (Republican)
1953-1959: Goodwin Knight (Republican)
1959-1967: Pat Brown (Democrat)
1967-1975: Ronald Reagan (Republican)
1975-1983: Jerry Brown (Democrat)
1983-1991: George Deukmejian (Republican)
1991-1999: Pete Wilson (Republican)
1999-2003: Gray Davis (Democrat) (First Recalled)
2003-2011: Arnold Schwarzenegger (Republican)
2011-2019: Jerry Brown (Democrat)

The voters decide who holds these positions and quite often they are from a different political party than the governor's. All California plural executives:

1. are separately elected,
2. serve four-year terms,
3. terms start 1st Monday after January 1 after their election,
4. have a two-term limit,
5. are subject to recall and impeachment, and
6. vacancies are filled by the governor.

The balance of the governor's administration is made up mostly of political appointees. These appointees include the governor's cabinet, staff, a large, diverse number of directors and commissioners of agencies, departments, and various boards and commissions. The way our state constitution is written, the governor is responsible and accountable to the people for the performance of every member of the administration.

The **ORDER OF SUCCESSION** *is the descending order of who assumes the governor's office in the event of death, resignation, removal, or disability.* The order of succession for the governor of California is:

1. Lieutenant Governor
2. President Pro Tempore of the Senate
3. Speaker of the Assembly
4. Secretary of State
5. Attorney General
6. Treasurer
7. Controller

If there is a question about the governor's competence, an appointed commission petitions the State Supreme Court for its determination.

II. The Office of Governor

According to the state constitution, "The supreme executive power of this state is vested in the Governor."

Candidates for governor must meet these state requirements:

1. Citizen of the United States.
2. Qualified to vote.
3. California resident for at least 5 years immediately preceding the election.

Governor Jerry Brown

Before the 2018 Election, These Top Contenders Were Fighting for the Title of Governor

| Current Lt. Governor Gavin Newsom | Current Treasurer John Chaing | Former L.A. Mayor Antonio Villaraigosa |

GUBERNATORIAL *refers to anything having to do with the governor.* The gubernatorial powers are those held by the chief executive of the state. They include the following:

1. Head of State and Chief Executive
2. Legislative Leader (Budgeting Power)
3. Appointment Power
4. Judicial Influence
5. The Power to Make Laws
6. Chief of State Security

www.governor.ca.gov

A. HEAD OF STATE AND CHIEF EXECUTIVE

Not only the most powerful government official of the state, the governor is also the world representative of California and its citizens. Ceremonial duties include ribbon-cutting, greeting world leaders, and other celebrations.

In addition to running the executive branch, the governor is also the leader of his or her political party, lending strength and prestige to that party.

Also, the governor can exercise influence by making appointments, nominations, and shaping the direction of state and local party organizations.

Even as the chief executive, the governor is limited by the plural executive created by the state constitution.

The governor sets policy priorities but shares responsibility for the day-to-day administration of the government with nearly a dozen other elected executive officers—each of whom may have his or her own agenda. So although the governor is held accountable for actions that affect the government, many times these actions are outside of his or her control.

The governor can greatly affect higher education because he or she is automatically the president of both the University of California Board of Regents and the California State University Board of Trustees.

Governor Brown's Concerns
State of the State Address 2017

Edmund G. Brown Jr., in the governor's annual "State of the State Address," referenced and focused on President Trump, explaining the influences the federal government may have on California's future. This was a departure from the usual focusing on a list of accomplishments.

"First," Brown said, "In California, immigrants are an integral part of who we are and they have helped create the wealth and dynamism of this state from the very beginning." **Trump is about immigrants.**

"I recognize that under the Constitution, federal law is supreme and that Washington determines immigration policy."

"But as a state we can and have had a role to play. California has enacted several protective measures for the undocumented: the **Trust Act**, lawful driver's licenses, basic employment rights, and non-discriminatory access to higher education.

"Second, more than any other state, California embraced the Affordable Care Act and over five million people now enjoy its benefits. But that coverage has come with tens of billions of federal dollars. Were any of that to be taken away, our state budget would be directly affected, possibly devastated." **Will Trump keep giving us federal funds for healthcare?**

"Third, our state is known the world over for the actions we have taken to encourage renewable energy and combat climate change. Whatever they do in Washington, they can't change the facts that temperatures are rising and so are the oceans and natural habitats everywhere are under increasing stress." **Will Trump allow California to remain the world leader in the fight against climate change?**

"Fourth is infrastructure. This is a topic where the President has stated his firm intention to build and build big." **Will Trump bring infrastructure to our state?** ▼

Trump said: "We will build new roads, and highways, and bridges, and airports, and tunnels, and railways all across our wonderful nation."

Brown said, "We can all work together—here in Sacramento and in Washington as well. We have roads and tunnels and railroads and even a dam that the President could help us with. And that will create good-paying American jobs."

The **TRUST ACT** (AB4) limits local jails from holding low-level, nonviolent, misdemeanor offenders for extra time just so they can be deported.

B. LEGISLATIVE LEADER (Budgeting Power)

The legislative leadership (budgeting power) is probably the most important power the governor possesses.

The governor is the **LEGISLATIVE LEADER** *of California because he or she presents a personal agenda and annual budget to the legislature and can exercise this leadership role with veto powers over legislation.* The governor can set **policy priorities** for California through proposed laws and through the budget. The governor can also call special elections and legislative sessions to deal with extraordinary matters.

On January 10 of each year, the governor presents to the legislature a proposed annual state budget.

The is done in conjunction with the **DEPARTMENT OF FINANCE (DOF)**, *which serves as the Governor's chief fiscal policy advisor and whose chief duty is to promote long-term economic sustainability and responsible resource allocation through the state's annual financial plan.*

The **STATE OF THE STATE ADDRESS** *is an annual speech presented by the governor to a joint session of the California legislature, typically delivered annually at the end of January.* The address not only reports on the condition of the state but also allows the governor to outline his legislative agenda, concerns, and state priorities. The address fulfills one of the expected "head of state" duties by the governor. An annual state budget covering projected revenues and expenditures is prepared and submitted to the legislature. After the legislature passes its version of the budget back to the governor, the governor may reduce or eliminate particular budget items by use of the line item veto.

The governor has veto power over legislation.

A revised budget bill is seldom signed "as is" by the governor. The *LINE-ITEM VETO allows the governor to eliminate specific items and amounts from the proposed budget that are not to the governor's liking.* The biggest legislative weapon the governor holds is the full veto. A *VETO is the total rejection of any bill that can then only be overridden by a two-thirds vote of both the state assembly and the state senate, as opposed to a simple majority (51%).* As a practical matter, a gubernatorial veto is difficult to override.

With a supermajority, the legislature can override any gubernatorial veto.

The constitutional revision of 1966 (extending time for legislative sessions) and the legislative re-organization of 1972 (continuous two-year session) effectively eliminated the pocket veto. A *POCKET VETO means that a governor fails to take any action on pending legislation after the legislature has adjourned.*

C. APPOINTMENT POWER

The governor has appointment power over departments and key policy makers. Several hundred of these appointments are for important board members and commissioners.

When a vacancy occurs due to death, removal, or resignation, the governor also makes appointments to fill the unexpired terms of the following offices:

1. Statewide officers
2. U.S. Senators
3. U.S. House of Representatives
4. County Supervisors
5. Judicial vacancies on the Superior Courts
6. State Supreme Court and Courts of Appeal Justices

D. JUDICIAL INFLUENCE

The governor has judicial influence through his or her power to nominate judges to the State Supreme Court, the Courts of Appeal, and fill vacancies by appointment as they arise. With regard to convicted felons, the governor has the power to pardon, commute sentences, and grant reprieves, but the reason for granting clemency must be reported to the

legislature. *CLEMENCY is the governor's power to reduce or eliminate the sentences of convicted felons for humanitarian reasons.*

The governor has the power of clemency unless the offender was convicted twice of a felony, then clemency requires recommendation of the California Supreme Court, with four judges concurring.

The governor may grant a *PARDON, which is the release of the convicted criminal from the legal consequences of the crime.* A governor may commute the sentence. *COMMUTE means a reduction in the length of a prison term. A REPRIEVE allows the governor to postpone a sentence of the court from being carried out.* A reprieve is only a delay and not a reduction of sentence, commutation, or pardon.

Without a doubt, the most controversial clemency power is the right of the governor to affect capital offenses. A *CAPITAL PUNISHMENT offense is one where the death penalty is prescribed by the court for the crime of taking, or involvement in the taking of, a human life.*

California voted on two competing initiatives concerning capital punishment. Prop 62 (see page 74) would have abolished the death penalty (as would have Prop 34), but it was rejected by a 54-46 margin. The other initiative, Prop 66, provides the streamlining of the capital crime appeal process, and also requires death row offenders to work in jail and pay restitution to victims' families, something from which they were previously exempted. The measure passed 51-49.

E. CHIEF OF STATE SECURITY

The governor is commander-in-chief of the state's **National Guard** and the **California State Military Reserve (CSMR),** which was formed to provide California a trained and organized military force in the event of a state security emergency when the National Guard is deployed. The governor can call the guard to active duty on his or her own initiative or upon the request of local officials in the event of a civil disturbance or natural disaster.

F. THE POWER TO MAKE LAWS

Bills that have been approved by both houses of the legislature are sent to the governor for his or her signature. The governor has 12 days after receiving the bill to do one of the following:

1. Sign the bill thereby making it a law.
2. Approve without a signature.
3. Veto the bill.

Remember: If two-thirds of both houses override the governor's veto, the bill becomes law.

III. Administration of the Executive Branch

There are many levels to the executive branch, making it resemble a giant corporation. There are thousands of people and many levels of management (see **Figure 6-1**).

A. THE EXECUTIVE BRANCH APPOINTMENTS

1. Governor's Cabinet
2. Agencies
3. Departments
4. Divisions
5. Governor's Personal Staff *

(* The staff does not have to be confirmed by the Senate.)

B. THE GOVERNOR'S CABINET

The *GOVERNOR'S CABINET is an advisory group that provides the chief executive with a comprehensive overview of state operations and has a hand in policy making and long-term planning for California.* Cabinet members must be confirmed by the state senate.

C. AGENCIES, DEPARTMENTS, AND DIVISIONS

The administrators of these agencies are referred to as "secretaries of the agencies." The secretaries of the agencies provide leadership to the departments so that the governor can communicate efficiently between the numerous departments. The members of the governor's cabinet are usually secretaries of the agencies.

Figure 6-1

California State Government...

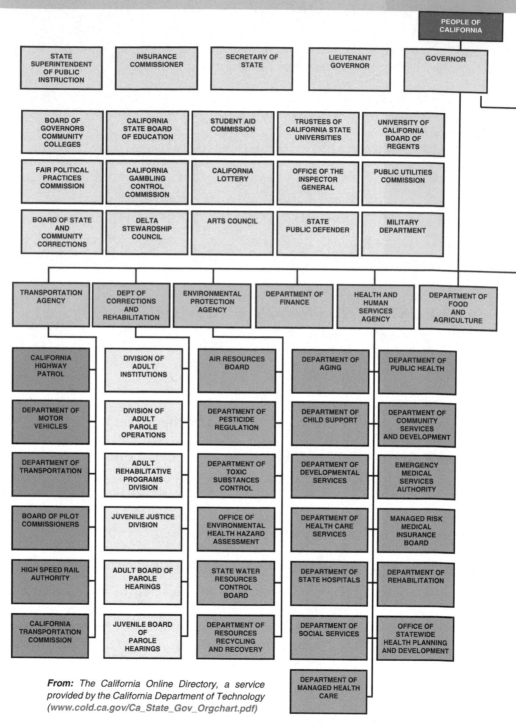

From: *The California Online Directory, a service provided by the California Department of Technology (www.cold.ca.gov/Ca_State_Gov_Orgchart.pdf)*

The Executive Branch

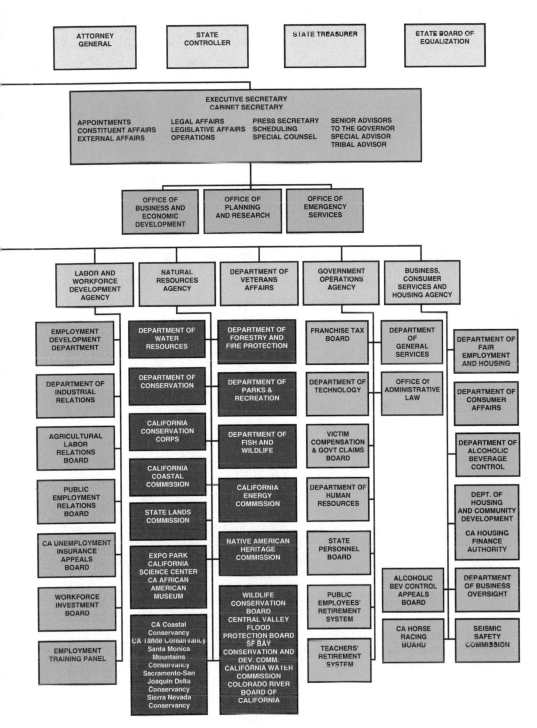

ATTORNEY GENERAL

STATE CONTROLLER

STATE TREASURER

STATE BOARD OF EQUALIZATION

EXECUTIVE SECRETARY
CABINET SECRETARY

APPOINTMENTS
CONSTITUENT AFFAIRS
EXTERNAL AFFAIRS

LEGAL AFFAIRS
LEGISLATIVE AFFAIRS
OPERATIONS

PRESS SECRETARY
SCHEDULING
SPECIAL COUNSEL

SENIOR ADVISORS
TO THE GOVERNOR
SPECIAL ADVISOR
TRIBAL ADVISOR

OFFICE OF BUSINESS AND ECONOMIC DEVELOPMENT

OFFICE OF PLANNING AND RESEARCH

OFFICE OF EMERGENCY SERVICES

LABOR AND WORKFORCE DEVELOPMENT AGENCY

NATURAL RESOURCES AGENCY

DEPARTMENT OF VETERANS AFFAIRS

GOVERNMENT OPERATIONS AGENCY

BUSINESS, CONSUMER SERVICES AND HOUSING AGENCY

EMPLOYMENT DEVELOPMENT DEPARTMENT

DEPARTMENT OF WATER RESOURCES

DEPARTMENT OF FORESTRY AND FIRE PROTECTION

FRANCHISE TAX BOARD

DEPARTMENT OF GENERAL SERVICES

DEPARTMENT OF FAIR EMPLOYMENT AND HOUSING

DEPARTMENT OF INDUSTRIAL RELATIONS

DEPARTMENT OF CONSERVATION

DEPARTMENT OF PARKS & RECREATION

DEPARTMENT OF TECHNOLOGY

OFFICE Of ADMINISTRATIVE LAW

DEPARTMENT OF CONSUMER AFFAIRS

AGRICULTURAL LABOR RELATIONS BOARD

CALIFORNIA CONSERVATION CORPS

DEPARTMENT OF FISH AND WILDLIFE

VICTIM COMPENSATION & GOVT CLAIMS BOARD

DEPARTMENT OF ALCOHOLIC BEVERAGE CONTROL

PUBLIC EMPLOYMENT RELATIONS BOARD

CALIFORNIA COASTAL COMMISSION

CALIFORNIA ENERGY COMMISSION

DEPARTMENT OF HUMAN RESOURCES

DEPT. OF HOUSING AND COMMUNITY DEVELOPMENT

CA UNEMPLOYMENT INSURANCE APPEALS BOARD

STATE LANDS COMMISSION

NATIVE AMERICAN HERITAGE COMMISSION

STATE PERSONNEL BOARD

CA HOUSING FINANCE AUTHORITY

WORKFORCE INVESTMENT BOARD

EXPO PARK CALIFORNIA SCIENCE CENTER CA AFRICAN AMERICAN MUSEUM

WILDLIFE CONSERVATION BOARD CENTRAL VALLEY FLOOD PROTECTION BOARD SF BAY CONSERVATION AND DEV. COMM. CALIFORNIA WATER COMMISSION COLORADO RIVER BOARD OF CALIFORNIA

PUBLIC EMPLOYEES' RETIREMENT SYSTEM

ALCOHOLIC BEV CONTROL APPEALS BOARD

DEPARTMENT OF BUSINESS OVERSIGHT

EMPLOYMENT TRAINING PANEL

CA Coastal Conservancy CA Tahoe Conservancy Santa Monica Mountains Conservancy Sacramento-San Joaquin Delta Conservancy Sierra Nevada Conservancy

TEACHERS' RETIREMENT SYSTEM

CA HORSE RACING BOARD

SEISMIC SAFETY COMMISSION

D. GOVERNOR'S PERSONAL STAFF

The *PERSONAL STAFF OF THE GOVERNOR is a group of approximately 100 coordinators who assist the governor in a variety of activities with the press, media, legislators, budget analysts, and others.* Usually they were the governor's closest advisors when he or she was a private citizen. Unlike the governor's cabinet, the personal staff is not confirmed by the state senate.

IV. California's Plural Executive (Voter Elected, Not Appointed)

There are seven state elected officers other than the governor and the five board of equalization members, all of whom make up the plural executive.

A. LIEUTENANT GOVERNOR   www.ltg.ca.gov

The **LIEUTENANT GOVERNOR** *is elected independently from the governor.*

Under California's Constitution, the Lieutenant Governor serves as Acting Governor whenever the Governor is absent from the state, and automatically becomes Governor if a vacancy occurs in the Office of Governor.

The Lieutenant Governor is **President of the Senate** and votes in case of a tie.

The Lieutenant Governor serves as both a voting member of the Board of Regents of the University of California and the Board of Trustees of the California State University system.

The Lieutenant Governor also serves on, and rotates with the State Controller, as chair of the three-member *STATE LANDS COMMISSION, which oversees the control and leasing of millions of acres of state-owned land, including offshore oil resources, as well as use and permitting for all navigable waterways in California.* The Commission also manages state land-use planning and revenues, and related interstate issues. During alternate years, when the Lieutenant Governor serves as Chairperson of the State Lands Commission, he also serves as a member of the **California Ocean Protection Council.**

Lieutenant Govenor Newsom Pushes to Make State Colleges "Sanctuary Campuses"

In the wake of Donald Trump's presidential win, students at universities across the country and in California have started a "Sanctuary Campus" movement, in addition to Sanctuary City movement.

President Trump, who won the election based in part on his promised tough immigration policies, has stirred up fears among some who believe his administration will deport undocumented immigrant students in the United States.

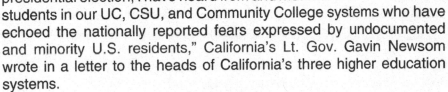

"In the week since Donald Trump's victory in the presidential election, I have heard from and met with students in our UC, CSU, and Community College systems who have echoed the nationally reported fears expressed by undocumented and minority U.S. residents," California's Lt. Gov. Gavin Newsom wrote in a letter to the heads of California's three higher education systems.

Newsom, who sits on the UC Board of Regents, while campaigning for the 2018 gubernatorial race, proposed the state make all of its UC, CSU, and community college campuses "Sanctuary Campuses."

What exactly is a "Sanctuary City/County"? At the local government-level, it means a city or county has adopted policies that limit local law enforcement's cooperation with federal immigration authorities. Similarly, a "Sanctuary Campus" is meant to prevent any university or college from assisting federal authorities in deportation efforts of undocumented students.

In Newsom's letter, he also said California's higher education systems should look to protect student data from "abuse by the Federal Government."

U. S. Attorney General Jeff Sessions made President Trump's immigration policies clear. The justice department plans to award $4.1 billion in grant money this year,but sanctuary cities will no longer be eligible to receive them. Any jurisdiction seeking or applying for DOJ grants will have to certify compliance with U.S. Code 1373 as a condition of receiving those awards. This is in reference to a U.S. law which says cities cannot prevent federal authorities from enforcing immigration laws.

In addition, under state statutes, the Lieutenant Governor chairs the *CALIFORNIA COMMISSION FOR ECONOMIC DEVELOPMENT*, *which provides support and guidance to the Governor, Legislature, and private sector regarding the development of California's economy.* The Lieutenant Governor is also a member of the State Job Training Coordinating Council and the California Emergency Council.

B. ATTORNEY GENERAL   *www.oag.ca.gov*

The *ATTORNEY GENERAL is the state's top lawyer and law enforcement official, protecting and serving the people and interests of California through a broad range of duties.* The Attorney General's responsibilities include safeguarding the public from violent criminals, preserving California's spectacular natural resources, enforcing civil rights laws, and helping victims of identity theft, mortgage-related fraud, illegal business practices, and other consumer crimes.

Overseeing more than 4,500 lawyers, investigators, sworn peace officers, and other employees, the Attorney General:

1. Represents the People of California in civil and criminal matters before trial courts, appellate courts, and the supreme courts of California and the United States.

2. Serves as legal counsel to state officers and, with few exceptions, to state agencies, boards and commissions.

3. Assists district attorneys, local law enforcement, and federal and international criminal justice agencies in the administration of justice.

4. Strengthens California's law enforcement community by coordinating statewide narcotics enforcement efforts, supporting criminal investigations and providing forensic science services, identification and information services, and telecommunication support.

5. Manages programs and special projects to detect and crack down on fraudulent, unfair and illegal activities that victimize consumers or threaten public safety.

Under the state constitution, the Attorney General is elected to a four-year term in the same statewide election as the Governor, Lieutenant Governor, Controller, Secretary of State, Treasurer, Superintendent of Public Instruction, and Insurance Commissioner.

California voters imposed a two-term limit on statewide offices.

The office of the Attorney General is often a stepping-stone to governorship. Examples include: Earl Warren (1942); Edmund "Pat" Brown (1958); and George Deukmejian (1982).

C. STATE CONTROLLER   www.sco.ca.gov

As the chief fiscal officer of California, the sixth largest economy in the world, the **STATE CONTROLLER** *is responsible for accountability and disbursement of the state's financial resources.* The Controller also safeguards many types of property until claimed by the rightful owners, independently audits government agencies that spend state funds, and administers the payroll system for state government employees and California State University employees.

The Controller (the numbers' guy) serves on 78 boards and commissions with authority ranging from state public land management to crime victim compensation.

The Controller is a member of numerous financing authorities, and fiscal and financial oversight entities including the Franchise Tax Board and Board of Equalization.

The Controller also serves on the boards of the nation's two largest public pension funds: the California State Teachers' Retirement System (CalSTRS) and the California Public Employees' Retirement System (CalPERS).

The Controller is one of eight statewide constitutional officials who are elected every four years in California. (In some states, this government official is called a "Comptroller.")

D. TREASURER   www.treasurer.ca.gov

The office of California State Treasurer has broad responsibilities and authority in the areas of investment and finance.

The **TREASURER** *is elected statewide every four years. In addition to being the state's lead asset manager, banker, and financier, the Treasurer serves as chairperson or a member of numerous state authorities, boards and commissions.* Below are some of the Treasurer's key responsibilities:

1. The Treasurer's Office manages the State's **POOLED MONEY INVESTMENT ACCOUNT**, *which invests monies on behalf of state government and local jurisdictions to help them manage their fiscal affairs.*

2. The Treasurer serves on the boards of the Public Employees' Retirement System and State Teachers' Retirement System. The **CALIFORNIA PUBLIC EMPLOYEES' RETIREMENT SYSTEM (CALPERS)** *is an agency in the California executive branch that manages pension and health benefits for more than 1.6 million California public employees, retirees, and their families.*

   The **CALIFORNIA STATE TEACHERS' RETIREMENT SYSTEM (CALSTRS)** *provides retirement, disability and survivor benefits for California's 868,493 prekindergarten through community college educators and their families.* CalPERS and CalSTRS invest their funds anticipating growth and are significant stockholders in both the American and global economies. The pension funds provide for the retirement of their members and also perform a variety of other services for them. As an example, CalPERS (public employees) is the second largest purchaser of health care services in the country.

Unfortunately, many public employees (CalPERS and CalSTRS) benefits are "unfunded," meaning there is not enough money to meet their promised benefits.

3. The Treasurer's Office finances a variety of important public works needed for the state's future, including schools and higher education facilities, transportation projects, parks, and environmental projects.

4. The Treasurer chairs authorities that finance a wide range of significant projects, including pollution clean-up, small businesses and health care facilities. The Treasurer chairs the state commission that awards low-cost, tax-exempt financing for various purposes such as housing, economic development, and student loans.

5. The Treasurer plays a key role in statewide housing finance as Chair of the Tax Credit Allocation Committee that awards hundreds of millions of dollars in tax credits for affordable housing and as a member of the Board of the California Housing Finance Agency, which finances affordable housing.

6. The Treasurer oversees the **ScholarShare Investment Board (SIB)**, which administers the state's tax-advantaged college tuition savings plan.

E. SECRETARY OF STATE   www.sos.ca.gov

The **SECRETARY OF STATE** *serves as the official record keeper of the acts of the legislature and the various executive departments as well as the supervisor of all state elections.* He or she maintains the state archives and is the keeper of the Great Seal of California, which must be affixed to all documents signed by the governor. All businesses, counties, and cities are granted incorporation charters by the Secretary of State. Most importantly, the Secretary of State must: enforce the state's election laws, print state ballot pamphlets, certify and publish election results, and check for the proper number of signatures on petitions for initiative, referendum, and recall.

In addition, he or she must collect and approve statements of campaign donations and expenses.

Many feel that the office of Secretary of State should be nonpartisan because of the involvement in the conducting of elections and the approval of campaign contributions.

The Secretary of State's responsibilities include:

1. Serving as the state's Chief Elections Officer.
2. Implementing electronic filing and Internet disclosure of campaign and lobbyist financial information.
3. Maintaining business filings.
4. Commissioning notaries public.
5. Operating the Safe at Home confidential address program.
6. Maintaining the Domestic Partners and Advance Health Care Directive Registries.
7. Safeguarding the State Archives.
8. Serving as a trustee of the California Museum.

F. SUPERINTENDENT OF PUBLIC INSTRUCTION

www.cde.ca.gov/eo

The **SUPERINTENDENT OF PUBLIC INSTRUCTION** *is the director of the California Department of Education (CDE) as well as the State Board of Education and is the **only nonpartisan officer** of the plural executive.* The superintendent sits as an ex officio member of more than one hundred

educated-related boards and commissions. **EX OFFICIO** *means that the holder of one office is automatically the holder of the second office.*

The CDE oversees the state's diverse and dynamic public school system, which is responsible for the education of more than seven million children and young adults in more than 9,000 schools. The CDE and the State Superintendent of Public Instruction are responsible for enforcing education law and regulations; and for continuing to reform and improve public elementary school programs, secondary school programs, adult education, some preschool programs, and child care programs. The CDE serves our state by innovating and collaborating with educators, schools, parents, and community partners, preparing students to live, work, and thrive in a highly connected world.

The CDE's mission is to provide a world-class education for all students, from early childhood to adulthood.

G. INSURANCE COMMISSIONER www.insurance.ca.gov

The **INSURANCE COMMISSIONER** *is responsible for overseeing the massive California Department of Insurance (CDI), as a whole, and for the approval of all future auto insurance rate increases.*

The CDI was created in 1868 as part of a national system of state-based insurance regulation. The insurance marketplace has changed dramatically over time, but consumer protection continues to be the core of CDI's mission.

Today, CDI is the largest consumer protection agency in the state. California is the largest insurance market in the United States and the sixth largest insurance market in the world.

The protection of consumers is at the heart of CDI's functions, including overseeing insurer solvency, licensing agents and brokers, conducting market conduct reviews, resolving consumer complaints, and investigating and prosecuting insurance fraud.

Consumers, insurance companies, and licensees rely on CDI to ensure that insurance products and services are available to consumers in a timely way, and that they deliver fair and equal benefits.

H. STATE BOARD OF EQUALIZATION www.boe.ca.gov

The *STATE BOARD OF EQUALIZATION (BOE) is the five-member governmental body that is responsible for the assessment of all property in California* (see Chapter 10).

Established in 1879 by a constitutional amendment, the BOE was initially charged with responsibility for ensuring that county property tax assessment practices were equal and uniform throughout the state.

Currently the tax programs administered by the BOE are concentrated in four general areas:

1. Sales and use taxes
2. Property taxes
3. Special taxes
4. The tax appellate program

The state is divided into four districts. An elected member from each district serves on the board along with the State Controller, who serves ex officio.

The four Board of Equalization districts are:

District One	**Northern California**
District Two	**Central California**
District Three	**Central Los Angeles Area**
District Four	**South-Eastern California**

V. Recent Governors

Most of the following nine governors were elected for at least two terms and deserve recognition because of the impact they had or continue to have.

Earl Warren "The Nonpartisan Advocate"
1943-1953 (Three terms) Republican-Democrat

Earl Warren was so popular that he is the only governor in California history elected for three consecutive terms. In his second term he won both the Republican and Democratic nominations under the old cross-filing system (which has since been abolished). He pushed for reforms in worker's compensation, prison conditions, and old-age pensions, but

referred to them as progressive, not liberal ideas. He resigned in 1953 and was appointed Chief Justice of the U.S. Supreme Court by President Dwight D. Eisenhower.

Goodwin Knight "Goodie"
1953-1959 (One term) Republican

Goodwin Knight served as Lt. Governor under Earl Warren, succeeding to the office of Governor in 1953 when Warren resigned. During his term, Knight made major achievements in the area of water conservation and development, including the beginning of the Feather River Project. He also improved the prisons and created the Department of Alcoholic Beverage Control.

Edmund "Pat" Brown "The First Brown"
1959-1966 (Two terms) Democrat

Edmund G. Brown faced controversy over the pressing state problems of water development, smog control, and capital punishment. By the end of his second term as governor, the state had greatly increased its spending. He more than doubled the miles of freeways, increased the State University and University of California Systems, and began the huge State Water Project.

Ronald Reagan "The Conservative"
1967-1974 (Two terms) Republican

Ronald Reagan, a former actor, excellent speaker, and a conservative who did not like "big government spending," won the governorship easily. Although taxes and spending went up slightly while he was governor, he cut and trimmed the budget where he could. Reagan supported "law and order" but had trouble reforming welfare programs. His popularity carried him into the Presidency of the United States for two terms.

Edmund "Jerry" Brown Jr. "The Non-traditionalist"
1975-1982 (Two terms)

Jerry Brown was a non-traditional governor, interested in the quality of life. Brown, an environmentalist, wanted alternative energy sources. He was against Proposition 13, the property tax reduction initiative, but supported it when it passed. That was the major factor in his landslide re-election in 1978.

George Deukmejian "The Uninteresting Conservative"
1983-1990 (Two terms) Republican

"Duke," as the press called him, was a conservative who was mostly interested in keeping the cost of government down. He took the responsibility of proposing a balanced budget very seriously. During his eight-year tenure as governor, he used his veto authority 4,000 times because the legislature was consistently trying to spend more money than was available.

Pete Wilson "Growth Problem Handler"
1991-1999 (Two terms) Republican

Pete Wilson was a moderate republican who was on a mission to handle, or at least minimize, California's population growth problems. The challenge of increasing highway, school and prison construction, while trimming state funded services and increasing funding by raising taxes, did not win him any popularity contests.

Wilson believed California's growth pains must be solved or improved if we are to continue to accommodate the anticipated population growth and yet remain competitive. One of his priorities was keeping California businesses from leaving the state.

Gray Davis "The Recalled Governor"
1999 to 2003 (Two terms) Democrat

This once popular governor became a victim of electricity shortages and rolling blackouts in the summer of 2001 which contributed to a massive increase in state debt. Although re-elected to a second term in 2002, he was recalled on October 7, 2003. (He became the first governor to be recalled in California history.)

Arnold Schwarzenegger "The Governator"
2003 to 2011 (Two terms) Republican

Arnold Schwarzenegger announced his candidacy in the 2003 California recall election for Governor of California on the August 6, 2003 episode of The Tonight Show with Jay Leno. On October 7, 2003, the recall election resulted in Governor Gray Davis being removed from office with 55.4% of the Yes vote in favor of a recall Schwarzenegger was elected Governor of California under the second question on the ballot with 48.6% of the vote to choose a successor to Davis. Because of his personal wealth from his acting career, Schwarzenegger did not accept his governor's salary of $175,000 per year.

Schwarzenegger's early victories included repealing an unpopular increase in the vehicle registration fee as well as preventing driver's licenses being given out to illegal immigrants, but later he began to feel the backlash when powerful state unions began to oppose his various initiatives.

Governor Schwarzenegger played a significant role in opposing Proposition 66, a proposed amendment of the Californian Three Strikes Law, in November 2004. This amendment would have required the third felony to be either violent or serious to mandate a 25-years-to-life sentence. In the last week before the ballot, Schwarzenegger launched an intensive campaign against Proposition 66. He stated that "it would release 26,000 dangerous criminals and rapists."

Although he began his tenure as governor with record high approval ratings (as high as 89% in December 2003), he left office with a record low 23%, only one percent higher than that of Gray Davis's when he was recalled in October 2003.

Edmund "Jerry" Brown Jr.
2011- 2019 (Two terms) Democrat

Brown was elected to a third term in 2011 and a fourth term in 2014, the only person to repeat as governor in California. During Brown's third term, he signed a historical package of groundwater legislation. The plan will regulate local agencies and also implement management plans to achieve water sustainability within 20 years.

His stated goals for his unprecedented fourth term in office were to construct the California High-Speed Rail, to create tunnels to shore up the state's water system, and to curb carbon dioxide emissions.

VI. California - Is Secession Possible?

Because California wields so much power (the sixth largest economy in the world), many members of the plural executive have been encouraging the change of California to that of an independent nation—in other words, seceding from the United States. The executive branch is particularly keen on the idea since President Trump took office—California is the polar opposite politically from the current Republican-controlled federal government.

Seceding from the union would allow the state to govern itself and join international treaties and organizations.

Secession Idea Moves Forward in California

SECESSION *in the United States properly refers to State secession, which is the withdrawal of one or more States from the Union that* constitutes the United States; but may loosely refer to leaving a State or territory to form a separate territory or new State, or to the severing of an area from a city or county within a State.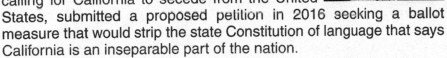

The "**Yes California Independence Campaign**," calling for California to secede from the United States, submitted a proposed petition in 2016 seeking a ballot measure that would strip the state Constitution of language that says California is an inseparable part of the nation.

The group first proposed the secession idea in 2014, but the so-called "**CalExit**" movement gained serious traction on social media after Republican Donald Trump won the presidential election. Secession backers are now collecting voter signatures to get a measure on the 2019 state ballot which, if passed, would help clear a path for legal secession.

The Attorney General's Office will review the request and submit language for a title and summary that would allow the group to begin collecting signatures for an initial referendum.

Threats and aspirations to secede from the United States, or arguments justifying secession, have been a feature of the country's politics almost since its birth. Some have argued for secession as a constitutional right and others as from a natural right of revolution. In *Texas v. White*, the United States Supreme Court ruled unilateral secession unconstitutional, while commenting that revolution or consent of the States could lead to a successful secession.

The most serious attempt at secession was advanced in the years 1860 and 1861 as eleven southern states each declared secession from the United States, and joined together to form the Confederate States of America.

A 2008 Zogby International poll found that 22% of Americans believed that "any state or region has the right to peaceably secede and become an independent republic."

VII. Chapter Summary

California has a **"plural" executive branch**, meaning that less power is concentrated in a single chief executive. The governor works with eleven other elected officials, each running a separate part of the government. Unlike the governor's appointees and cabinet members, these plural executives will often represent different political parties than the governor. They include the Lieutenant Governor, Attorney General, Controller, Secretary of State, Treasurer, Superintendent of Public Instruction, Insurance Commissioner, and the five members of the Board of Equalization.

Jerry Brown, the Governor of California, has several important roles. He is the ceremonial leader of the state, greeting important dignitaries and representing California to the nation and the rest of the world. The governor is also **the leader of his political party** in California. He makes **appointments to key state offices and commissions**. The governor also **nominates judges** to the state supreme court, as well as filling vacancies on some of the lower courts. The governor has the power to grant **clemency** to convicted felons, giving **full pardons**, **commuting** a sentence, or granting **reprieves**. The governor is automatically the **Commander-in-Chief of the state militia**, calling the National Guard to active duty at will.

The governor's most important responsibility is that of **legislative leader**. The governor's office prepares a **state budget** to accomplish these goals and submits it to the legislature for approval. The legislature makes its adjustments and passes the budget back in the form of an **appropriations bill**. The governor then has the option of approving the budget, or reducing and eliminating specific budget items by using the **"line item veto."**

The governor has line item veto power over any bill passed by the legislature. It takes a **two-thirds vote** of both the assembly and the senate to override a gubernatorial veto. If the governor signs a bill, it becomes law.

The **Lieutenant Governor** has few significant duties. The **Attorney General** is legal counsel for the state and director of the justice department, responsible for the fair enforcement of California's laws. The **State Controller** is the state's chief accountant and the chair of the

Franchise Tax Board. The **Superintendent of Public Instruction**, a nonpartisan post, directs the **Department of Education**. The **Secretary of State** is California's official record keeper, recording all acts of the legislature and overseeing elections. The **State Treasurer** is responsible for supervising the bonds we issue to finance huge public works projects for the state. The **Insurance Commissioner** oversees the massive California insurance industry. The **State Board of Equalization** has four members plus the state controller. They are responsible for assessing real estate for tax purposes. They also collect sales taxes and taxes on cigarettes, gasoline, and alcohol.

VIII. Class Discussion Questions

1. Which one of the plural executives has no daily assigned tasks and why?

2. What is the difference between the governor's powers regarding clemency, pardon, commute and reprieve?

3. How can the governor trim a budget bill without the help and cooperation of others?

4. Which of our recent governors served multiple terms?

5. Which one of our governors became Chief Justice of the U.S. Supreme Court? President of the United States?

Chapter 7

The California State Legislature: Our Lawmakers

The State Assembly, the State Senate, and several other agencies and departments compose the Legislative Branch of the California State Government. This branch holds the principal lawmaking powers of the state. On average, the Legislature will propose, analyze, and debate over 6,000 bills in a single two-year session.

The California Legislature, as the representative of the people, has the responsibility of making the laws and controlling the state's money. California has a **BICAMERAL** *legislature. It is made up of two houses: the state senate and the state assembly.* The **state senate is referred to as the "upper house"** and consists of only 40 members, and the **state assembly is referred to as "lower house"** and consists of 80 members.

I. How the State Legislature Functions

The main purpose of the legislature is:

1. Making State Laws
2. Establishing Taxes
3. Confirmations
4. Placing Constitutional Amendments on the Ballot
5. Spending State's Money (Appropriations)
6. Oversight

www.legislature.ca.gov

Chapter Outline

The legislature also has the right to:

1. Establish courts
2. Maintain public schools
3. Executive powers (non-legislative power)
4. Judicial powers—including impeachment (non-legislative power)
5. Constituent powers (constitution making and the amendment process)

The legislature has all of those powers that the state constitution does not grant exclusively to the executive or judicial branches of the state's government or its local units, and neither the state constitution nor the United States Constitution denies to the legislature.

A. LEGISLATIVE PROCESS

The legislative process in Sacramento begins with a bill (**see chart on next page**). A *BILL is a draft of a law presented to the state senate or state assembly for approval or rejection.* Once a bill has been introduced by a member of one of the houses, it is sent to a legislative committee for study and revision. If it gains committee approval, the bill is sent to the floor of that house for a vote by the entire membership. Eventually, a majority in each house must agree on the bill before it is sent to the governor. See the chart on the next page.

B. BILLS NEXT GO TO THE GOVERNOR

The governor, after receiving a bill, has 12 days in which to sign, not sign, or veto it. If the governor signs or does not take any action on the bill, it becomes law. If the governor vetoes the bill it is dead, unless two-thirds of the members in each house vote to override the veto.

C. THE LEGISLATURE MAY OVERRIDE A VETO

The legislature may override the governor's veto. A *VETO OVERRIDE means that the legislature can make laws, even if the governor vetoes a bill, by obtaining the required two-thirds vote of the members in each house.* In recent history, Governor Edmund "Jerry" Brown Jr., during his first two terms (1975-1982), vetoed about 10% of all bills sent to him, causing a large number of veto overrides.

How a Bill Makes Its Way Through

Introduction

Legislator sends idea for a bill to the **Office of the Legislative Counsel**, where it is drafted into bill form. The draft of the bill is returned to the legislator for introduction. If the author is a Senator, the bill is introduced in the Senate. If the author is an Assembly Member, the bill is introduced in the Assembly.

First Reading

A bill's first reading is when the clerk reads the bill number, the name of the author, and the descriptive title of the bill. The bill is then sent electronically to the Office of State Printing. A bill must be in print for **30 days**, giving time for public review, before it can be acted upon.

Committee Hearings

After introduction, a bill goes to the **Senate or Assembly Rules Committee,** where it is assigned to the appropriate policy committee for its first hearing.

Bills are assigned to policy committees according to subject area.

The public may attend legislative committee hearings.

During the committee hearing the author presents the bill to the committee, and testimony may be heard in support or opposition to the bill.

Bills may be amended several times. The committee can pass the bill, pass the bill as amended, or defeat the bill.

Bills that require the **expenditure of funds** must also be heard in the fiscal committees, Senate Appropriations, and Assembly Appropriations. Each committee is made up of a specified number of Senators or Assembly Members.

Second Reading

Bills passed by committees are read a second time in the house of origin and then placed in the **Daily File** for a third reading.

Third Reading

Bill analyses are also prepared prior to third reading. When a bill is read the third time, it is explained by the author, discussed by the Members, and voted on by a roll call vote.

Bills that require an **appropriation,** or that take effect immediately, ordinarily require **27 votes in the Senate** and **54 votes in the Assembly** to be passed.

the Legislative Process

Other bills generally require **21 votes in the Senate** and **41 votes in the Assembly**.

If a bill is defeated, the Member may seek reconsideration and another vote.

> **Repeat
> Process in
> Other House**

Once the bill has been approved by the house of origin, it proceeds to the other house where the procedure described above is repeated.

> **Resolution of
> Differences**

If a bill is amended in the second house, it must go back to the house of origin for concurrence, meaning agreement on those amendments.

If the house of origin does not concur in those amendments, the bill is referred to a two-house conference committee to resolve the differences. Three members of the committee are from the Senate and three are from the Assembly.

If a compromise is reached, the bill is returned to both houses for a vote.

> **Governor**

If both houses approve a bill, it goes to the Governor. The Governor has three choices: sign the bill into law, allow it to become law without his or her signature, or veto it. A governor's veto can be overridden by a two-thirds vote in both houses.

Most enacted bills go into effect on the **first day of January of the next year**. Urgency bills, and certain other measures, take effect immediately after they are enacted into law.

> **California
> Law**

Bills to become law are sent to the Secretary of State for final review.

Source: *Friends Committee on Legislation of California (FCLCA.org)*

D. LEGISLATIVE SESSIONS

The legislature meets in time periods referred to as sessions. The *GENERAL SESSION is a two-year period that starts at noon on the first Monday in December, during even-numbered years, and ends on November 30 of the next even-numbered year.* With the passage of the "term limits" initiative (two terms, eight years total for state senators and three terms, six years total for assembly members), the careers of legislators can best be described as "temporary full-time professionals."

E. BUDGET BILL

Each year before January 11, the governor must submit a proposed budget for consideration to the senate and assembly. The budget bill must be enacted in both houses by midnight, on June 15, annually. This deadline has not always been met in the past.

A *SPECIAL SESSION can be called by the governor to deal with urgent matters.* Legislative action is limited to only the subject specified by the governor.

REAPPORTIONMENT is the process of dividing districts into groups that are approximately equal in population. This process is also called re-mapping, mapping, redistricting, or districting. The principle of equal-elective representation **requires districts to be redrawn at the beginning of each decade** to conform to changes in population. *GERRYMANDERING is the process of redrawing district lines to increase the number of seats held by the majority party.* Both of these were previously under legislative control.

To avoid gerrymandering, California voters passed both Prop 11 and Prop 20, which created an independent redistricting organization called the **California Citizens Redistricting Commission.** This commission determines the boundaries for the state and U.S. Senate, state assembly, U.S. House of Representatives, and the state Board of Equalization (BOE).

F. CONSTITUTIONAL AMENDMENT

The legislature, by the passage of a constitutional amendment, was provided with a direct method of amending the state constitution. If two-thirds of the membership of each house concur, the legislature can submit a constitutional amendment directly to the people by simply placing it on the ballot where it must then be ratified by a majority of the voters.

G. OVERSIGHT

Certain committees in the legislature perform an oversight function. *OVERSIGHT COMMITTEES act as watchdogs to make sure legislation, or programs that have been passed by the legislature, are being carried out properly by the employees of the executive branch. They also review the efficiency of programs to see if these programs can be accomplished more economically.*

When an oversight committee's investigation reveals a severe impropriety, the state constitution allows the legislature to proceed with impeachment. *IMPEACHMENT is the process by which the legislature formally charges an elected official with misconduct.* The assembly must first vote for the articles of impeachment before they can be sent to the senate. The elected official is then tried in the senate where a two-thirds vote of the full membership is necessary to remove the official.

These severe measures, however, are rare. In general, oversight is not as exciting or glamorous for legislators as introducing bills or handling constituency problems, but it is a vital function of a bureaucracy in order to help make for an effective and efficient government.

H. CONFIRMATIONS

CONFIRMATION is the process in the state senate of either approving or rejecting, by a majority vote, the hundreds of appointments made by the governor. Confirmation hearings are held for the heads of the governor's cabinet, commissions, boards, and even the director of the Department of Motor Vehicles. The senate rules committee holds hearings on the fitness of all the nominees and makes a recommendation to the full membership of the senate. If the full senate approves a candidate by a simple majority vote, the candidate is confirmed. The assembly does not play an active role in the confirmation process, although the candidate does need a two-thirds approval vote from the assembly as well as the senate.

II. California Senate

A. CALIFORNIA SENATE (Upper House)

The Senate has been in Democratic hands continuously since 1970.

www.senate.ca.gov

Requirements for Legislators

ELIGIBILITY – At least 18 years of age.

RESIDENCY – California resident for three years, at least one year in the district (immediately prior).

TERM LENGTH – Assembly, 2 years; Senate, 4 years.

TERM LIMIT – 12 years (combined) in the Assembly and/or Senate.

SENATE SEAT ROTATION – 20 seats each even-numbered year.

ASSEMBLY SEAT ROTATION – All 80 seats even-numbered years.

CODE OF ETHICS – Binds both houses—may expel a member by two-thirds vote.

COMPENSATION – **Leaders:** $111,776 annually plus a per diem of $168. **Legislators:** $97,197 annually plus a per diem of $168. Telephone and gasoline expense allowance for a state-licensed automobile. Limited health and retirement benefits.

The *CALIFORNIA SENATE is the upper house in the legislature with 40 members serving four year-terms (two term limit), with half of the senate districts conducting elections every two years.* The U.S. Supreme Court requires the upper house of a state legislature to be based on population rather than the geographic size of the county. This has resulted in a shift of more senate seats to Southern California.

The senate has, for many years, been more stable, less partisan, and more conservative in its procedures than the assembly. Each senator represents over 887,500 people. The number of senators has been set by the state constitution at 40, exactly half the size of the state assembly.

B. SENATE LEADERSHIP

According to our state constitution, the *LIEUTENANT GOVERNOR is automatically the ex officio president of the senate but, in actuality, this is largely a ceremonial post.* He or she has no role of note in senate matters unless there is a rare 20-20 vote, then the lieutenant governor provides the tie-breaking vote.

The powerful *SENATE PRESIDENT PRO TEMPORE is the member elected by the senate to be its leader.* Since the lieutenant governor is rarely present during most sessions, the leadership of the upper house is vested in the Senate President Pro Tempore. Chosen by fellow senators, the "Pro Tem" is the one who presides over the senate.

The *SENATE RULES COMMITTEE is chaired by the Senate President Pro Tempore, and includes four other members elected by the senate.* This committee has the power to appoint all the other senate committee chairs and vice-chairs. The senate rules committee is also extremely powerful in that it decides which committee will be assigned to each bill coming up for consideration. It also selects the senators who will serve on executive and judicial boards and commissions.

The *MAJORITY AND MINORITY FLOOR LEADERS are senate members appointed by their party to direct the party's political strategy in the legislature.*

C. THE PRESTIGE OF THE SENATE

The senate chamber is decorated in deep reds—the traditional color of the upper class—and with good reason. The "upper house," with its small number of representatives and longer term, is more select—and, therefore, more prestigious—than the assembly. If an assembly member has a chance to win election to the senate, he or she will usually do so. But now that we have term limitations, don't be surprised if you see senate members switch to the assembly—and vise-versa—just to remain in the legislature for a few more terms.

III. California Assembly

A. CALIFORNIA ASSEMBLY (Lower House)

The *CALIFORNIA STATE ASSEMBLY is the lower house in the legislature with 80 members serving two-year terms (three term limit).* The assembly is known for its power struggles and is generally more volatile than the senate.

 www.assembly.ca.gov

B. ASSEMBLY LEADERSHIP

The powerful *SPEAKER OF THE ASSEMBLY is the presiding officer of the assembly, elected by the membership and automatically serving (ex officio) on all assembly and joint legislative committees.* His or her powers parallel those of the president pro tempore, the counterpart in the senate. The speaker

names a member of his or her political party to be the majority floor leader. But the entire assembly elects an Assembly Speaker Pro Tempore, who runs the proceedings during the speaker's absence. The speaker also chairs the assembly's rules committee. This important position allows the speaker to control the flow of legislative activity on the floor—in much the same way that the senate's rules committee chair (the pro tem) controls the legislative business of that house.

The *MAJORITY PARTY FLOOR LEADER is appointed by the speaker to represent the majority party*. The *MINORITY PARTY FLOOR LEADER is chosen by, and represents, the minority party*. The minority floor leader is also called the "minority whip."

IV. Committee System

The legislature does all of its work by the use of the committee system. A *COMMITTEE SYSTEM is a system whereby the legislature is broken down into smaller committees; a basic working component that can study all bills in depth.* Most new bills are first referred to one of the standing committees for in-depth study and review.

A. THE DIFFERENT TYPES OF COMMITTEES

The *RULES COMMITTEES are powerful committees that refer all bills to standing committees, as well as selecting and supervising the assembly support staff.* It is chaired in the senate by the pro tem, and in the assembly by the speaker.

STANDING COMMITTEES are the basic, or core, committees that will do most of the work for the current session and are established by the rules of each house at the beginning of each session. There are currently 28 established standing committees in the assembly and 25 in the senate. Good old-fashioned politics determines who controls these committees and what the exact membership will be during each session. Each committee is assigned bills, according to its jurisdiction, which it will hear, study, hold public hearings on, change as needed, and finally vote on in committee.

In addition to the standing committees in each house, the legislature also employs joint committees. *JOINT COMMITTEES are committees consisting of an equal number of assembly members and senators who study subjects of mutual interest to both houses.* They recommend legislation that they believe will be acceptable to both houses.

Assembly Standing Committees

Accountability and
   Administrative Review
Aging and Long-Term Care
Agriculture
Appropriations
Arts, Entertainment, Sports,
   Tourism, and Internet Media
Banking and Finance
Budget
Business, Professions, and
   Consumer Protection
Education
Elections and Redistricting
Environmental Safety and
   Toxic Materials
Governmental Organization
Health
Higher Education
Housing and Community
   Development

Human Services
Insurance
Jobs. Economic Dvelopment,
   and the Economy
Judiciary
Labor and Employment
Local Government
Natural Resources
Public Employees,
   Retirement, and Social
   Security
Public Safety
Revenue and Taxation
Rules
Transportation
Utilities and Commerce
Veterans Affairs
Water, Parks, and Wildlife

FISCAL COMMITTEES are standing financial committees that oversee the annual state budget and handle all other bills that either directly or indirectly involve a cost to the state.

CONFERENCE COMMITTEES are set up to resolve differences between the assembly and the senate versions of the same bill.

SELECT OR SPECIAL COMMITTEES are set up by either house to research limited subject areas where the forming of a permanent standing committee may not be seen as necessary.

V. Legislators' Salary and Benefits

Both chambers of the California Legislature receive the same base salary of $97,197 a year and, when the legislature is in session, a $168 tax-free per day (per diem) living expense allowance. Six legislative leaders receive a larger salary ($111,776) because of their additional responsibilities. All legislators receive round-trip travel expenses to and from legislative sessions and

committee meetings, gas and telephone credit cards, and use of a state-licensed auto. This salary, including perks, makes them the highest paid legislators in the country.

VI. Types of Legislation

A. BILLS AND RESOLUTIONS

There are basically two types of legislation: bills and resolutions. The most important type, as discussed earlier, is a bill. Most of the work done by the legislature is expressed in the form of bills. The state budget and state taxes are no exception. New budgets and taxes are discussed, revised, and approved or rejected as bills. The majority of California's bills pass through the legislature according to the procedure described in "Legislative Process." Two special kinds of bills, however, follow different rules.

An *APPROPRIATION BILL is one that authorizes funds to be spent from state revenues. URGENT BILLS are bills that must take effect immediately after being enacted.* These two types of bills require a two-thirds approval of each house.

Bills are assigned numbers so that they can be identified easily. Assembly bills have an (AB) before each number and (SB) is placed before a senate bill.

The second type of legislation is the resolution. A *RESOLUTION is a vote on a matter that involves one house, or in some instances both the assembly and senate, but does not require the governor's approval.* There are four kinds of resolutions:

CONSTITUTIONAL AMENDMENT – known as **ACA** or **SCA**, depending on the house of origination. A constitutional amendment is a resolution to change our state's constitution. An amendment must pass by a two-thirds majority in each house before it can be placed on the next election ballot. It must be ratified by a majority of those voting before the constitution can be changed.

CONCURRENT RESOLUTION – known as **ACR** or **SCR**, depending on the house of origination. This is used to adopt joint rules, establish joint committees, and congratulate groups or individuals. A simple majority of each house is needed to pass a concurrent resolution.

What Does the Democratic Two-Thirds Supermajority Mean for California?

Broadening the path to long-sought deals on affordable housing, transportation, infrastructure, and climate change, California Democrats have again captured a two-thirds supermajority in both houses of the Legislature.

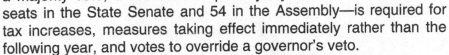

While most legislation in Sacramento needs only a majority vote, a two-thirds supermajority—27 seats in the State Senate and 54 in the Assembly—is required for tax increases, measures taking effect immediately rather than the following year, and votes to override a governor's veto.

This may be "bad news" for the Governor and for the (California) Republican party, because the California Assembly and California Senate, working together, has the potential to pass certain legislation without their approval.

The California Assembly and California Senate, as a **two-thirds supermajority**, may have enough voting power to:

1. Approve tax increases,
2. Suspend legislative rules,
3. Pass emergency legislation, or
4. Overturn the governor's vetoes without any support from Republicans.

However, Democrats won't be able to pass things on a supermajority unless all Democrats agree. This is due to the fact that moderate Democrats and pro-business Democrats may not align themselves with liberal Democrats.

While it's unlikely many Republican bills will become law, Republicans will still be able to influence which Democratic bills make it through, and which don't—they will still play a role in being able to deny or provide votes for important bills.

The last time the legislature was able to override a California governor was during Brown's first term after being elected in 1980.

What Have Been the Effects of Term Limits in California?

Until 1996, there were no term limits in California. Lawmakers could serve as long as their constituents kept electing them.

From 1996 to 2012, legislators could serve up to six years in the Assembly (three terms) and eight years in the Senate (two terms), with a lifetime limit of 14 years in the legislature. Voters approved this plan in 1990 when they passed **Proposition 140**.

In 2012, voters passed **Proposition 28**, which limited legislators to a total of 12 years of service, which can be served in one house or in both houses.

The Governor and all other statewide officers, except the Insurance Commissioner, can serve two terms of four years, with a limit of two terms. This constitutional limitation was passed in November 1990.

Presently, 15 states have term limits for legislators. In all, 21 states have passed legislative term limits at one time or another, but the limits have been repealed or declared unconstitutional in six of those states.

How have term limits affected Sacramento's policy-making processes? In both houses, committees now screen out fewer bills assigned to them and are more likely to see their work rewritten at later stages. The practice of "hijacking" Assembly bills—gutting their contents and amending them thoroughly in the Senate—has increased sharply, although the passage of **Proposition 54** (legislative transparency) may change that.

What brought about the death of the peer-to-peer relationship between the governor and legislative leaders? In the first half of the 1990s, budget debates in Sacramento were a duel of wits between then-Governor Pete Wilson and then-Assembly Speaker Willie Brown. The two were a year apart in age; Brown entered the Legislature in 1964, one class ahead of Wilson. With each possessing three decades of political smarts, they punched at the same weight.

JOINT RESOLUTION – known as AJR or SJR, depending on the house of origination. This action urges the U.S. Congress to pass or defeat legislation currently before it. In this way the state legislature lets its opinion be known regarding national issues.

HOUSE RESOLUTION – known as AR or SR, depending on the house of origination. A house resolution is used to create one-term committees, amend rules of that house, and congratulate groups and individuals. These resolutions are usually adopted by a voice vote of the majority.

B. TRACKING LEGISLATION (Bills)

A person can receive a free copy of a current bill, as it goes through the legislature, by simply going to the "bill room" in the basement of the state capitol building in Sacramento.

With the huge number of bills introduced in each two-year legislative session, both houses publish guides to help keep interested people informed. The *DAILY FILE is an agenda of that day's business*, whereas the *DAILY JOURNAL contains an account of the preceding day.*

In addition to these guides, histories are published by each house. There is *DAILY HISTORY, WEEKLY HISTORY, SEMIFINAL HISTORY, a FINAL HISTORY and a LEGISLATIVE INDEX of the entire two-year legislative session. These all summarize the actions taken on bills during this period.*

C. LEGISLATIVE TRANSPARENCY

In recent years, most candidates have promised "more legislative transparency," but it has been hard to see any action that would imply an increase in transparency.

Prop 54 has set new standards for our California legislature regarding legislative transparency (see the box on the next page).

VII. Legislative Staff

A. EMPLOYEES

The legislature of California has one of the largest staffs in the United States. Each legislative member is entitled to an administrative assistant and secretaries for both his or her capital office and also the district office.

Prop 54 - Legislative Transparency

The California Constitution requires legislative meetings to be open to the public, except when certain matters are being discussed. Live video of most, but not all, meetings is available on the state legislature's website. About $1 million is spent per year recording, posting, and storing videos. Under current law, there is no time regulation of when legislators can vote on a bill.

Prop 54 requires the following:

1. Prohibits legislature from passing any bill unless it has been in print and published on the Internet for at least 72 hours before the vote, except in cases of public emergency.

2. Requires the legislature to make audiovisual recordings of all its proceedings, except closed session proceedings, and post them on the Internet.

3. Authorizes any person to record legislative proceedings by audio or video means, except closed session proceedings.

4. Allows recordings of legislative proceedings to be used for any legitimate purpose, without payment of any fee to the state.

Prop 54 was passed by the voters in the November 2016 election.

B. JOINT STAFF

The **LEGISLATIVE COUNSEL** (*www.leginfo.ca.gov*) *is the chief legal counsel for the legislature, which is selected at the beginning of each session by the agreement of both houses.* Most bills are prepared by the legislative counsel's office. This counsel advises the legislature on the legality and constitutionality of measures and prepares indexes of the California codes and statutes. The **LEGISLATIVE ANALYST** (*www.lao.ca.gov*) *provides the legislature with financial, economic, and fiscal advice. He or she is appointed by the joint legislative budget committee.* The staff of the legislative analyst's office evaluates every item in the proposed state budget and all bills (appropriation bills) requiring money that go before the fiscal (revenue and expenditure) committee. Most importantly, the legislative analyst prepares a financial analysis of each proposition to be included in the state ballot pamphlet.

Part-time or Full-time Legislature in California?

Being a legislator in California was relatively easy before the last recession hit. Tax money stopped flowing and the legislature was not prepared to react to a depleted treasury.

Many voters in California believe that our current legislature is dysfunctional and out of touch with the real world. It appears that our legislators would rather score political points instead of solving California's myriad of problems. Would changing our legislature from full-time to part-time resolve this?

Only nine states in the United States have full-time legislatures—California, Illinois, Massachusetts, Michigan, New Jersey, New York, Ohio, Pennsylvania, and Wisconsin.

In 1966, California went from a part-time legislature to a full-time legislature hoping to create a more professional body who could do a better job of governing a complex state. It appears that instead of creating a stronger legislative body, we have created full-time politicians who have never worked a real job like most Californians.

Many Californians believe that our legislators cannot relate to our daily problems as a state because they have never had to deal with the same situations personally. A return to a part-time legislature would give our lawmakers in Sacramento a chance to work real jobs and understand the impact of the laws they make.

California's legislators make some of the highest salaries in the nation. As a part-time legislature, their salary and per diem would be cut in half, saving our financially-strapped state money.

Texas is a good example of a part-time legislature. Their legislature meets every other year for 140 days and creates a biennial budget. If an emergency situation comes up, the governor can call a for a special, limited session that can last up to 30 days.

If California were to switch back to a part-time legislature, would lawmakers be forced to get the job done in the limited time they have? Many argue that full-time legislatures have too much time on their hands to create and pass laws that are not necessary.

The *AUDITOR GENERAL is appointed by the joint legislative audit committee to assist the legislature by examining, auditing, and reporting on the financial statements submitted by the executive branch.*

VIII. Media Coverage

A. CAL-SPAN

The California assembly (lower house) televises its proceedings live on cable television. *CAL-SPAN is the nonprofit company that distributes the signal to a statewide cable system available to over two million subscribers.*

B. C-SPAN – NATIONAL COVERAGE

C-SPAN, the nation's television programmer for the federal government, is very successful. It is so successful that it broadcasts "full-time coverage" of all types of events that are affected by federal policy. Its reports are entirely objective and nonpartisan.

C. NEWSPAPERS AND NEWS SERVICES

Californians are kept up-to-date on political news from Sacramento by reading newspapers (see **Figure 7-1**) and periodicals, listening to the radio, and watching network programming or cable coverage. Since Sacramento, the capital, is the political news center, many newspapers, news services, magazines, and newsletters maintain capital bureaus.

D. THE INTERNET AND SOCIAL MEDIA

With an increasing dissatisfaction of the **main stream media (MSM)**, more and more people (especially young people) are going online for their news, including alternate media news sites, Facebook, Twitter, etc.

As the Internet is growing in popularity for younger readers, many established "printed" newspapers are struggling to maintain subscribers. Some have "gone under" while others have focused on maintaining or increasing their relevance by creating an online presence.

Figure 7-1

Daily Newspapers in California

Los Angeles Times - Los Angeles

San Jose Mercury News - San Jose

The Sacramento Bee - Sacramento

The Orange County Register - Santa Ana

The San Diego Union-Tribune - San Diego

San Francisco Chronicle - San Francisco

Contra Costa Times - Walnut Creek

Investor's Business Daily - Los Angeles

La Opinión - Los Angeles

The Press-Enterprise - Riverside

San Francisco Examiner - San Francisco

San Gabriel Valley Tribune - Monrovia

The Daily Breeze - Torrance

The Modesto Bee - Modesto

Los Angeles Daily News - Woodland Hills

The Press Democrat - Santa Rosa

Long Beach Press-Telegram - Long Beach

Inland Valley Daily Bulletin - Rancho Cucamonga

The Tribune - San Luis Obispo

Chico Enterprise-Record - Chico

Santa Monica Daily Press - Santa Monica

Santa Barbara News-Press - Santa Barbara

The Monterey County Herald - Monterey

Daily Press - Victorville

Glendale News-Press - Glendale

Merced Sun-Star - Merced

Lodi News-Sentinel - Lodi

Napa Valley Register - Napa

The Daily Californian - Berkeley

The Stanford Daily - Stanford

The Salinas Californian - Salinas

Red Bluff Daily - Red Bluff

Redlands Daily Facts - Redlands

Manteca Bulletin - Manteca

Bakersfield Californian - Bakersfield

Asbarez - Los Angeles

Appeal-Democrat - Marysville

Oakland Tribune - Oakland

The Desert Sun - Palm Springs

The Porterville Recorder - Porterville

Redding Record Searchlight - Redding

The Daily Independent - Ridgecrest

San Mateo County Times - San Mateo

San Mateo Daily Journal - San Mateo

Santa Clarita Valley Signal - Santa Clarita

Santa Cruz Sentinel - Santa Cruz

The Record - Stockton

Ventura County Star - Ventura

The Daily Democrat - Woodland

Visalia Times - Delta/Tulare

Advance-Register - Visalia

IX. Chapter Summary

The California State Legislature is patterned after the national legislature in Washington, D.C. It is a **"bicameral"** legislature that consists of two houses: the State senate and the State assembly. The **senate** (or upper house) has forty members. The **assembly** (or lower house) has eighty. **Bills** are drafts of proposed legislative action. They are used by the legislature to create new laws, approve the spending of money, or to permit the legislature to raise money through taxes. A bill must be approved by a majority of both houses before it can be passed on to the governor for approval. Certain bills and resolutions (such as **appropriations bills, urgent bills**, and **constitutional amendments**) require a **two-thirds majority vote** in each house to be approved. **Resolutions** are legislative votes on matters that do not require the governor's approval.

Senate members serve four-year terms and assembly members serve two-year terms. Under term limitations, senators may serve for eight years (two terms) while assembly members serve for no more than six years (three terms). To hold a legislative seat, a person must be at least 18 years old and be a California resident for at least three years (living in the represented district for at least one year).

With only forty members, the **state senate (or upper house)** is more prestigious than the **assembly**. Each senator represents more than 887,500 citizens. The **Lieutenant Governor** is the ceremonial president of the senate, but the real leader is the senate **President Pro tempore**. The pro tem is elected by the senate and is the counterpart to the **Speaker of the Assembly**. He or she controls the flow of legislation, makes important committee appointments, and chairs the powerful **senate rules committee** (comparable to the **rules committee in the assembly**). The **pro tem** controls the purse strings of the state, since the rules committee must approve all expenditures. Each party also appoints a **majority** or **minority floor leader**.

The presiding officer of the assembly is the **speaker**. The speaker is elected by the members, and serves on all **joint legislative committees**. This very powerful position dominates the legislature, controlling the flow of legislative activity, controlling the size and membership of all the committees, and appointing committee chairs and other important posts. The speaker appoints the **majority party floor leader** to represent his or her party during the session. The minority party also has its own **floor leader**. A **speaker pro tempore** (or pro tem) is selected by the membership to run the day-to-day proceedings. The pro tem is an automatic member of the powerful **assembly rules committee**, but has no vote. The assembly rules committee is chaired by the speaker. It controls the flow of all bills through the assembly and also supervises the assembly support staff.

Each legislative session lasts **two years**, starting the first Monday in December on even numbered years and ending two years later on November 30. Every year the governor must submit a proposed budget by January 11. The legislature is required to work with the governor's budget and both houses must enact it by June 15. The governor calls a **"special session"** of the legislature to deal with a specific urgent matter.

The **California Citizens Redistricting Commission** determines the boundaries for the state and U.S. Senate, state assembly, U.S. House of Representatives, and the state Board of Equalization (BOE). This was previously the responsibility of the state legislature.

X. Class Discussion Questions

1. What does the state legislature do for us?

2. Why does a state senator have "more prestige"?

3. Why do the assembly speaker and the senate president pro tempore have so much power?

4. What is the difference between a bill and a resolution?

5. Term limitations had what effect on the legislators?

Chapter 8

Our Judicial System

General Court Information
www.courts.ca.gov/courts.htm

Most Californians have little direct contact with the state's judicial system, except for the occasional traffic ticket, but this system of courts is an essential part of our government.

The *CALIFORNIA JUDICIAL SYSTEM is the branch of the state government that administers justice under the law.* Unlike many other government operations, the judicial system is run primarily by the state. Ninety percent of all court cases filed in California are handled by our state courts. Federal law violations and state law claims which depend on some element of federal law can be heard in federal courts.

TRUMP ANXIETY

Will President Trump raise havoc with California state laws?

1. State courts challenge withholding of federal funds as retaliation for fighting Trump policies.

2. California has joined other states in federal court to oppose limitations on immigration.

3. Trump has power to impose the enforcement of federal laws (marijuana, for example).

Chapter Outline

The California court system—the largest in the nation, with more than 2,000 judicial officers, approximately 17,000 court employees, and nearly 8.5 million cases—serves over 39.8 million people.

The state constitution vests the judicial power of California in the Supreme Court, Courts of Appeal, and Superior Courts. The constitution also provides for the formation and functions of the Judicial Council, the policy making body for the judicial branch.

Our California judicial system consists primarily of our courts, but is supported by a network of agencies and departments working together. This network—representing not just the judicial branch, but the executive and legislative branches as well—includes the following groups:

1. Three-Level Court Structure (See **Figure 8-1**)
2. The Judicial Council
3. Commission on Judicial Appointments
4. Commission on Judicial Performance
5. Habeas Corpus Resource Center
6. State Bar of California

I. California's Three-Level Court Structure

California's judicial power is vested in three California state courts:

1. Supreme Court
2. Courts of Appeal
3. Superior Court

A. COURTS: EITHER TRIAL OR APPELLATE COURTS

The three-tier court system can be divided into two types of courts: trial and appellate. A *TRIAL COURT is a court where the facts are determined and a decision is made by a judge (or jury, if requested).* Superior Courts are primarily trial courts, but can also serve as Appellate Courts in certain narrow situations. An *APPELLATE COURT primarily determines whether the proper procedures were used in the original trial and whether the law was properly applied or interpreted.* The Courts of Appeal generally hear cases on appeal. The Supreme Court has discretion to review Courts of Appeal decisions.

All courts hear both civil and criminal cases.

CIVIL CASES relate to individual rights and usually seek monetary damages. The party filing a civil action is called the PLAINTIFF and the party defending

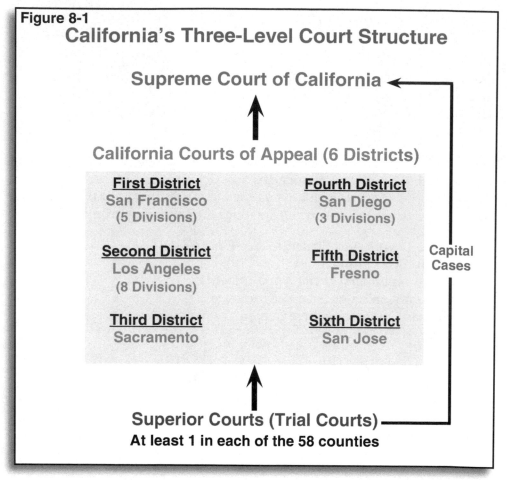

Figure 8-1
California's Three-Level Court Structure

Supreme Court of California ⬅

↑

California Courts of Appeal (6 Districts)

First District San Francisco (5 Divisions)	**Fourth District** San Diego (3 Divisions)
Second District Los Angeles (8 Divisions)	**Fifth District** Fresno
Third District Sacramento	**Sixth District** San Jose

Capital
Cases

↑

Superior Courts (Trial Courts)
At least 1 in each of the 58 counties

is called the **DEFENDANT**. A **JUDGMENT** states the amount of money or other relief for damages awarded by the judge or jury to the winner in a civil court case.

CRIMINAL CASES are brought by the State of California to punish violations of criminal laws.

D. SUPREME COURT OF CALIFORNIA

The Supreme Court of California is the state's highest court. It is made up of seven justices—the chief justice and six associate justices. When the Supreme Court decides to rule on a matter quickly, it may remove a case from a lower court and hear it directly.

The Supreme Court's decisions are binding on all other California courts. The court conducts regular sessions in San Francisco, Los Angeles, and

Governor Jerry Brown Nominates Yet Another Liberal State Supreme Court Justice

Although becoming a California State Supreme Court Justice involves a thorough approval and confirmation process, it begins with a nomination by the state governor.

Governor Brown in 2017 handpicked a justice, James Hume, that leaves no doubt as to the Governor's liberal leanings. He is the first openly gay man to serve on the California Supreme Court. Justice Hume is expected to tip the scales of justice firmly in the left-wing direction, adding that much more weight to a state with a liberal Democratic Governor, Senate, and Assembly.

Hume joined a very diverse court, considering Governor Brown's last three selections included a Taiwanese American former UC Berkeley law professor, a Mexican immigrant and Stanford University scholar, and an African American former federal government lawyer—all of whom were under the age of 50 when confirmed.

Four more picks could possibly be made by Governor Jerry Brown because of the advanced ages of the remaining State Supreme Court Justices.

It should come as no surprise that Brown has chosen to select a liberal justice to further tilt the state court as a means to challenge the actions of President Trump and the U.S. Supreme Court. President Trump's upcoming opportunity to appoint more conservative judges is expected to lean the U.S. Supreme Court even further to the right.

With every branch of California government now dominated by Liberal Democrats, how will it affect California's relationship with the national (more conservative) Republican powers? And with such a majority, how long will it be before another branch of the government sees a Republican stand a chance of attaining a position of power?

Sacramento and may also occasionally hold special sessions elsewhere. It has discretion to review Courts of Appeal decisions, which the parties petition to be reviewed.

The Supreme Court has discretionary review of decisions by the Commission on Judicial Performance to admonish, censure, or remove a judge for misconduct.

In an effort to keep political bias out of our courts, all judges in California are elected on a nonpartisan ballot.

The Supreme Court also reviews the recommendations of the **State Bar of California** concerning the disciplining of attorneys for misconduct.

All death row cases (capital cases) are automatically appealed to the Supreme Court for review.

The Supreme Court adopts rules governing the conduct of judges, both on and off the bench, and the conduct of judicial candidates in their campaigns. These rules are known as the **Code of Judicial Ethics**.

The only other matters coming directly to the Supreme Court are appeals from decisions of the **Public Utilities Commission**.

New justices of the State Supreme Court and the State Courts of Appeal are first nominated by the governor to 12-year terms and then must be confirmed by the Commission on Judicial Appointments. These judges are subject to retention elections for additional 12-year terms.

California Supreme Court
www.courts.ca.gov/supremecourt.htm

C. COURTS OF APPEAL

The **COURTS OF APPEAL** *primarily review trial court decisions to determine if legal error occurred and whether such error requires reversal.* There are six districts (see Figure 8-1) of the Courts of Appeal and a total of 105 justices who serve 12-year terms.

The legislature has constitutional authority to create new appellate districts and divisions.

Each district (or division, in the case of the First, Second, and Fourth Appellate Districts) has a presiding justice and two or more associate justices. Appellate justices are appointed by the governor and

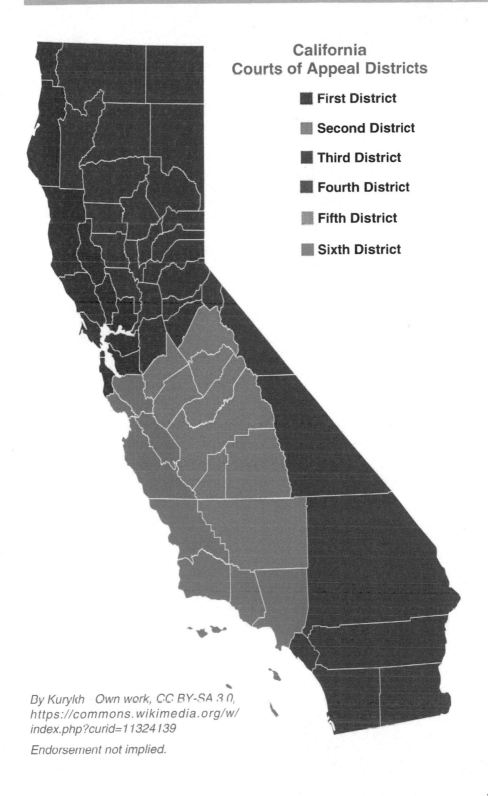

California
Courts of Appeal Districts

- First District
- Second District
- Third District
- Fourth District
- Fifth District
- Sixth District

confirmed by the Commission on Judicial Appointments. The same rules that govern the selection of Supreme Court justices apply to those serving on the Courts of Appeal.

California Courts of Appeal
www.courts.ca.gov/courtsofappeal.htm

D. SUPERIOR COURTS

The *SUPERIOR COURT is the state's basic civil and criminal trial court.* The court's case load is made up mainly of:

1. Civil cases, including personal injury cases,
2. Family law cases,
3. Guardianship cases,
4. Probate cases, and
5. Criminal cases.

The California Legislature determines the number of judges in each court. Superior Court judges serve six-year terms and are elected by county voters on a nonpartisan ballot at a general election. Vacancies are filled through appointment by the governor. A Superior Court judge must have been an attorney admitted to practice law in California or have served as a judge of a court of record in this state for at least 10 years immediately preceding election or appointment.

The Superior Court civil cases are divided into two categories; those that seek more than $25,000 (unlimited jurisdiction), and those that seek less than $25,000 (limited jurisdiction).

California Superior Courts
www.courts.ca.gov/superiorcourts.htm

1. Small Claims Courts

SMALL CLAIMS COURTS are separate courts for civil cases where the amount in question is $10,000 or less for an individual. The purpose of the Small Claims Court is to provide a speedy, inexpensive, informal method of settling claims without attorneys or usual legal procedure.

Small Claims Court
www.courts.ca.gov/selfhelp-smallclaims.htm

E. JUSTICES FACE ELECTION AFTER APPOINTMENT

To be eligible for appointment to the Superior Court, a person must have been a member of the State Bar of California or a judge of a court in this state for at least 10 years. **Superior Court judges are elected (not appointed) in nonpartisan elections for six-year terms and may be reelected to additional six-year terms**. In addition, all Superior Court judges, if appointed to fill emergency vacancies, must run for the balance of their terms at the next regularly scheduled general election. They must then run for reelection at the end of each term.

After the justices of the State Supreme Court and the State Courts of Appeal are nominated by the governor to 12-year terms, they must be confirmed by the **Commission on Judicial Appointments**. These judges are subject to retention elections for additional 12-year terms.

II. The Judicial Council of California and Other Judicial Branch Entities

A. JUDICIAL COUNCIL OF CALIFORNIA

Created in 1926 by constitutional amendment, and chaired by the Chief Justice, the *JUDICIAL COUNCIL OF CALIFORNIA is the policy-making body for California's state court system.*

The 21 voting members of the Judicial Council as established in the California Constitution consist of the Chief Justice, 14 judicial officers appointed by the Chief Justice, 4 attorney members appointed by the State Bar Board of Trustees, and 1 member from each house of the legislature. Council members do not represent any particular constituency but act in the best interests of the statewide judicial system and the public.

The council oversees the business operations of our state courts and reports its recommendations for improvement to the legislature and the governor. In addition, the judicial council addresses issues of racism, sexism, and language bias (against non-English speakers) in the courts. Most importantly, it plans for the future of the court system and its sources of funding.

B. COMMISSION ON JUDICIAL APPOINTMENTS

The *COMMISSION ON JUDICIAL APPOINTMENTS consists of three members who must confirm all judicial appointments for the California Courts of Appeal and Supreme Court.* The three members of the Commission on

171

Judicial Appointments are: the Chief Justice of the State Supreme Court, the Attorney General of California and a senior presiding Justice of the Courts of Appeal. Their job is to hold hearings where law enforcement officials, members of the state bar, and private citizens can express their opinions or concerns about qualifications of the chosen nominee.

No appellate appointment is final until the commission has filed its approval with the Secretary of State.

C. COMMISSION ON JUDICIAL PERFORMANCE

The *COMMISSION ON JUDICIAL PERFORMANCE is a commission of nine private citizens which deals with the censure, removal, retirement, or public or private admonishment of judges and commissioners for either misconduct or inability to perform their duties on account of permanent disability.* The Commission on Judicial Performance can recommend forced retirement or removal of any judge. The commission is composed of 11 members: one justice of a Court of Appeals and two judges appointed by the Supreme Court, four members appointed by the governor (two attorneys and two non attorney public members), two public members appointed by the Assembly Speaker, and two public members appointed by the Senate Rules Committee. Appointments are for four-year terms.

In California, there are four ways to remove a judge:

1. Normal election process.
2. Impeachment and conviction by the state legislature.
3. Recall election – called if 20% of the registered voters sign a recall petition.
4. Conviction of a felony or a crime of moral turpitude – must be recommended by commission on judicial performance.

D. HABEAS CORPUS RESOURCE CENTER

The *HABEAS CORPUS RESOURCE CENTER handles state and federal habeas corpus proceedings in death penalty cases and provides training and resources for private attorneys who take these cases.*

E. STATE BAR OF CALIFORNIA

The *STATE BAR OF CALIFORNIA, as authorized by the state constitution, is the professional organization that acts as the administrative arm of the Supreme Court in matters of attorney admission and discipline.* With nearly 250,000 members, the State Bar of California is by far the largest state bar in the country.

State law requires the State Bar's Commission on Judicial Nominees Evaluation to review the qualifications of persons being considered by the governor for appointment to the courts.

The State Bar of California
www.calbar.ca.gov/

F. CALIFORNIA CASES AND THE U.S. SUPREME COURT

Usually, the U.S. Supreme Court may only hear a case litigated in a lower federal court or in a state court if it involves an issue of federal law. The U.S. Supreme Court also determines whether a state constitution or state law conforms to the provisions of the federal constitution. The state courts are bound by its decisions. In most states, cases must go through the state Supreme Court before being submitted to the U.S. Supreme Court. In California, however, cases may also go to the U.S. Supreme Court directly from a California Court of Appeals.

Supreme Court Judge Neil Gorsuch is Trump's first appointment to the highest court, but how many more is the big question.

U.S. Senate Republicans approved Judge Neil Gorsuch, restoring the conservative majority on the U.S. Supreme Court. Justice Antonin Scalia's death led to a political standoff involving all three branches of government. His contentious confirmation was accomplished under the now famous "nuclear option" which allows Supreme Court nominees to be confirmed with only a simple majority vote. This was started by Ex-Senate majority leader Harry Reid, a Democrat from Nevada, who persuaded his fellow Democrats to approve the rule change because he was frustrated by the Republicans.

President Donald Trump's Travel Ban

Several States (mostly democratic) have joined lawsuits to challenge President Trump's temporary travel bans. The President has accused the judiciary of becoming "political" as his executive  orders have faced legal challenges in federal courts. The President further suggested that the Ninth Circuit Court was "overreaching" its authority.

III. Court Procedures

A. CRIMINAL CASES

After being arrested, the accused is brought before a judge, usually a Superior Court judge, to be arraigned. An **ARRAIGNMENT** *is the court procedure where the judge officially informs accused parties of their legal rights and the charges against them and provides an opportunity to enter a plea.* The judge sets the date for the arraignment hearing. Security given for the appearance of a prisoner is bail. **BAIL** *is the amount of money that must be posted to assure the accused is present at his or her court appearance.* If the accused is of little danger to the public, he or she can be released without bail, or, *"on his or her **OWN RECOGNIZANCE.**"*

Most criminal cases are resolved without a trial. Since trials are costly and time-consuming, the courts encourage plea bargaining. **PLEA BARGAINING** *is a negotiation between prosecutor and defendant, by which the defendant agrees to plead guilty to a lesser crime. It is a compromise between the two parties that allows the case to be finished quickly.*

In order to establish clear guidelines for punishment, crimes are grouped into three major categories: infractions, misdemeanors, and felonies. **INFRACTIONS** *are the least serious types of crimes, such as traffic violations (typically punishable by fines).* The punishment for an infraction is usually a fine and, in rare cases, jail time. **MISDEMEANORS** *are more serious crimes, including such acts as drunk driving or shoplifting that could be punishable by up to a year in jail.* Misdemeanor convictions carry fines and jail time of less than one year in prison. **FELONIES** *are the most serious types of crimes and include such crimes as grand theft auto, drug trafficking, and serious physical harm, including murder.* These crimes are punishable by prison terms of over a year and, under special circumstances, death.

Only about 25% of the cases are felony criminal cases—which must carry a possible jail term of a year or more—or juvenile delinquency problems.

An alternative to prison terms is probation. **PROBATION** *is the act of suspending the sentence of a convicted offender and giving the offender supervised freedom.*

B. JUVENILE OFFENDERS

JUVENILES *are people under the age of 18 and, because of this fact, are treated differently from adults in our legal system.*

Our society wants to protect the juvenile and itself at the same time. A juvenile is not sent to jail or prison, but rather to juvenile hall until his or her case is heard and, if convicted, will be sent to a detention center where society will try to rehabilitate that person.

C. CIVIL CASES

In a civil case, the procedure is simpler. The plaintiff files a complaint with the court clerk. A *COMPLAINT* is *the legal claim brought against the defendant.* The court then issues a summons for the defendant. The general procedures that follow issuance of the summons are: 1) the complaint is served on the defendant; 2) the defendant answers the complaint and/or summons or objects to the sufficiency of the complaint and may file a cross-complaint; 3) the parties engage in the discovery process to evaluate each other's evidence; and 4) the case is either settled or tried before a judge or a jury, which decides the merits of the case.

D. THE USE OF ALTERNATIVE DISPUTE RESOLUTION (ADR)

In the last decade, many standard contracts have included an **alternative dispute resolution (ADR)** clause (in writing or online) that requires the parties to mediate before proceeding to any court action. Since it can take a year for a court to hear a case, mediation seems like a good alternative.

Most Superior Court judges require the parties to hire a private judge to mediate a civil case first before the Superior Court judge will actually hear it in a courtroom. See **Figure 8-2** for a more detailed description of the ADR process.

IV. Attorneys in California

A. CITIZENS' RIGHT TO AN ATTORNEY

The California Constitution and the U.S. Constitution both provide that a person accused of a crime has the right to be represented by an attorney.

No person can practice law without first being admitted to the California State Bar.

B. PROSECUTING AND DEFENSE ATTORNEYS

The **DISTRICT ATTORNEY (D.A.)** is *the prosecuting attorney for the state government at the county level.* He or she evaluates the cases brought before the D.A.'s office and decides which cases should be filed and go to trial. As discussed earlier, few criminal cases actually go to trial. The cost to

Figure 8-2

ALTERNATIVE DISPUTE RESOLUTION (ADR) *is any method of resolving disputes other than by litigation.* Public courts may be asked to review the validity of ADR methods, but they will rarely overturn ADR decisions and awards if the disputing parties formed a valid contract to abide by them.

The most common types of ADR for civil cases are mediation, settlement conferences, evaluation by a neutral party, and arbitration. However, mediation and arbitration are most often used.

In ***MEDIATION****, an impartial person called a "mediator" helps the parties try to reach a mutually acceptable resolution of the dispute.* The mediator does not decide the dispute but helps the parties to settle the dispute themselves.

Mediation leaves control of the outcome with the parties.

Mediation may be particularly useful when parties have a relationship they want to preserve—for example, family members, neighbors, or business partners. Mediation is also effective when emotions are getting in the way of resolution.

In ***ARBITRATION****, a neutral person called an "arbitrator" hears arguments and evidence from each side and then decides the outcome of the dispute.*

Arbitration is less formal than a trial, and the rules of evidence are often relaxed.

Arbitration may be either "binding" or "nonbinding." ***BINDING ARBITRATION*** *means that the parties waive their right to a trial and agree to accept the arbitrator's decision as final.* Generally, there is no right to appeal an arbitrator's decision. ***NONBINDING ARBITRATION*** *means that the parties are free to request a trial if they do not accept the arbitrator's decision.*

Arbitration is best for cases where the parties want another person to decide the outcome of their dispute for them but would like to avoid the formality, time, and expense of a trial.

Why consider the use of ADR? ADR is usually less formal, less expensive, and less time-consuming than a trial. ADR can also give people more opportunity to determine when and how their dispute will be resolved.

Using ADR may have a variety of benefits, depending on the type of ADR process used and the circumstances of the particular case. Benefits of ADR may include:

1. **People Want to be Heard** - It gives them a chance to present their case and participate in its resolution.

2. **Reduced Conflict** - Mediation can lessen the conflict and any hostility that may often accompany a dispute.

3. **Quicker Resolution/Reduced Expense** - In mediation, disputes can often be resolved in a matter of weeks or months rather than the amount of time required in a lengthy court trial.

In a Judicial Council study of five mediation pilot programs for general civil cases, attorneys in cases that settled in mediation estimated that their clients saved almost $50 million in litigation costs over a two-year period. (www.courts.ca.gov/documents/empprept.pdf)

4. **Increased Satisfaction** - Because of these and other benefits, participants in mediation typically express very high satisfaction with the mediation process.

Mediation of Child Custody and Visitation Disputes

The legislature has mandated that trial courts provide mediation in family court cases where child custody or visitation is in dispute. Child custody mediation helps parents develop a parenting plan that resolves custody and visitation issues and results in an agreement more than half of the time. This reduces the acrimony that often exists and  can be very detrimental to children and parents when custody and visitation issues are adjudicated and allows a more efficient use of judicial resources.

Source: *California Courts - www.courts.ca.gov/programs-adr.htm*

"Three Strikes" More than Twenty Years Later

The Three Strikes law ensures that a person who commits a felony after a previous conviction of one or more serious felonies will be given an increased prison sentence and greater punishment. It includes as prior convictions certain felonies committed by older juveniles. The stated purpose of the law is to curb repeat criminal activity.

Since the enactment of the Three Strikes law in 1994, there have been a number of legal challenges, most significantly the constitutionality of the measure. Specifically, the Three Strikes law made it possible for a repeat offender to receive a prison sentence of 25 years to life for a nonserious or nonviolent felony (for example, petty theft with a prior), thereby raising legal questions about the federal Constitution's Eighth Amendment protection against cruel and unusual punishment. Related legal challenges also have argued that Three Strikes violates the "proportionality rule" in sentencing (the idea that "the time should fit the crime") because a relatively minor crime committed by a repeat offender could result in a much harsher punishment than a violent crime committed by a first-time offender.

While some court rulings have limited the law, other rulings have upheld most provisions of the law. As regards the issue of cruel and unusual punishment, the U.S. Supreme Court ruled in *Ewing v. California* that it is constitutional to sentence a repeat offender to an indeterminate life sentence for the commission of a nonserious or nonviolent felony. In *People v. Superior Court (Romero)*, the state Supreme Court ruled that Three Strikes did not eliminate judicial discretion to dismiss prior serious or violent felony convictions.

The major legal issues raised by challengers to the law seemed to have been addressed by the courts.

Legislative Analyst's Office (LAO)
www.lao.ca.gov/2005/3_strikes/3_strikes_102005.htm

the judicial system would be astronomical if every criminal case did go to trial. In most instances the district attorney will drop up to half of all felony charges and only prosecute the strongest cases where there is good, factual evidence.

The **DEFENSE ATTORNEY** *is the attorney for the accused.* A **PUBLIC DEFENDER** *is a county-employed attorney who represents the accused in a criminal case when the accused cannot afford private counsel.* Legal services for the indigent are also offered by such groups as Legal Aid.

V. Peace Officers

A **POLICE OFFICER** *is employed by a city and sworn to uphold justice.* The bulk of law enforcement work by the police is carried out at the street level. City police chiefs are usually appointed by the city manager or the police commission. The police officer's counterpart in the unincorporated county areas is called a sheriff's deputy.

A **SHERIFF** *is a peace officer who works for the county, runs the county jail, and provides a crime lab for the city police within that county if needed.* The County Sheriff, the top administrative officer, is elected through a nonpartisan election.

A **HIGHWAY PATROL OFFICER** *is a state peace officer who protects our safety on highways and state or county roads. The Highway Patrol also protects state buildings, the governor, and other state officials.*

A **MARSHAL** *is a county peace officer who runs the courtrooms, serves court-related legal papers, and physically evicts tenants if ordered.* His or her main job is to protect the judges.

VI. Citizens' Participation

Citizens can participate in the judicial system as witnesses, jury members, or grand jury members.

A **WITNESS** *is an individual who has seen something relevant to the commission of a crime.*

Proposition 63 Passes -
Regulation of Large Ammunition

California enacted legislation to regulate the sale of ammunition. The legislation requires individuals and businesses to obtain a one-year license from the California Department of Justice to sell ammunition. The legislation also requires sellers to conduct background checks of purchasers with the Department of Justice.

Proposition 63 required individuals who wish to purchase ammunition to first obtain a permit. The measure mandated dealers to check this permit before selling ammunition. The measure also eliminated several exemptions to the large-capacity magazines ban and increased the penalty for possessing them. Proposition 63 enacted a court process that attempts to ensure prohibited individuals do not continue to have firearms.

Proposition 47 of 2014 made stealing an item that is valued at less than $950 a misdemeanor. Therefore, stealing a gun valued at less than $950 is a misdemeanor. Proposition 63 made stealing a gun, including one valued at less than $950, a felony punishable by up to three years in prison.

In a *JURY TRIAL, a group of 12 (or fewer) men and women judges whether the accused (in a criminal case) is innocent or guilty of the charges, and in a civil case, which party prevails.* In civil trials, the number of jurors is reduced to eight if the parties stipulate to it. Jury members are selected from the county voter registration roll and DMV records.

Each of the 58 counties in California has a grand jury. A *GRAND JURY is a group of 19 citizens (23 in Los Angeles because of its large population) who investigate criminal activity and county government and issue reports to the public.* The grand jury, selected by the county's Superior Court judges, serves for a period of one year and acts as the county's "watchdog." At the end of that year, it must submit a final report to the county board of supervisors. The grand jury has the power, in unusual cases, to indict someone. An *INDICTMENT is a complaint against a person, charging that person with a crime.*

Correction and Rehabilitation

California used to have a prison population of 163,000 in facilities that were designed to hold about 85,000. By 2015, the inmate population had been reduced to 111,250, mainly due to the effects of Prop 47, which was passed in 2014. The measure's plan made all shoplifting, embezzlement, writing bad checks, and other theft crimes under $950 to be a misdemeanor (a far cry from the  $400 that had always made these crimes a felony charge). Other charges that are no longer felonies include most drug possessions. Under Prop 47, those charged with the misdemeanor crimes would receive a citation with a court date about one month away instead of being booked into jail on what would previously have been a felony count. California had hoped to reduce 40,000 felony convictions per year, which represents 1/5 of the annual convictions in the state.

Law enforcement officials and others have blamed Prop 47 for allowing repeat offenders to continue breaking the law with little consequence.

Crime has risen in the state's largest cities, setting off debate over whether the proposition is responsible. In some areas, street cops are making fewer narcotics arrests.

Finally, without the threat of a felony conviction and a lengthy stint behind bars, fewer drug offenders are enrolling in court-ordered treatment in Los Angeles and other counties.

California Department of Corrections and Rehabilitation
www.cdcr.ca.gov/

181

VII. Chapter Summary

California's judicial system is primarily a state (but does include federal) entity. It is a network of courts, agencies, and other groups including police departments, the state bar, and the prison and parole systems.

The California court system has three levels: Supreme Court, Courts of Appeal, and Superior Courts.

The **Supreme Court** is the highest court in the state. Its decisions are binding over all other courts. The Supreme Court, at its discretion, hears lower court appeals or may take a case directly from a lower court if it is felt to have constitutional significance. The court consists of a **Chief Justice** and six **Associate Justices**, each serving twelve-year terms. The governor appoints nominees to the Supreme Court and Courts of Appeal to 12-year terms. These judges are subject to retention elections for additional 12-year terms. **Superior Court judges are elected (not appointed) in nonpartisan elections for six-year terms and may be reelected to additional six-year terms**. All Supreme Court and Courts of Appeal appointments are reviewed and confirmed by a Commission on Judicial Appointments.

The U.S. Supreme Court will only hear a case from the state court if it involves federal constitutional issues. The federal court insures that state court rulings and laws passed by the state legislature conform to the U.S. Constitution.

Generally, appeals of disputed cases from lower or trial courts rise to the next level, the Courts of Appeal. These appellate courts re-examine cases to correct legal errors, not factual errors. There are **six District Courts of Appeal in California**.

The many **Superior Courts** primarily function as "trial" courts, handling civil cases and divorce proceedings, guardianship petitions, probates, and some serious criminal and juvenile offenses. Superior Court judges are chosen in nonpartisan elections for six-year terms.

Small Claims Courts are a type of lower court specializing in simple civil cases where the judgment amount is currently $10,000 or less for individual cases.

Criminal cases are categorized as either **infractions** (minor crimes), **misdemeanors** (more serious crimes), or **felonies** (very serious crimes). **Plea bargaining** is an agreement between the prosecutor and defense attorney to accept a plea of guilty to a lesser crime. Such arrangements ease congestion in the courts, as the accused is convicted without the need of a trial.

Alternative Dispute Resolution (ADR) is becoming a more and more attractive method to avoid having to go to court.

Some convicted offenders are allowed to serve their prison sentences on **probation**.

In a criminal case, the **district attorney** is the prosecuting attorney for the government at the county level. In civil cases, the state of California is the party filing a court action, while the defendant is the person or entity being sued or charged with a crime. The **defense attorney** represents the defendant. In a criminal case, this will often be a **public defender** if the defendant cannot afford an attorney.

After being arrested, an accused person is entitled to an **arraignment** before a judge where he or she is formally made aware of the charges and given an opportunity to enter a plea. At this point the individual may be held in custody, released on bail (as set by the judge), or released on his or her own **recognizance**.

In civil cases (usually over money damages), the **plaintiff** files a case against the **defendant**, who is summoned to court and responds to the complaint. Both sides conduct **discovery** and present the **evidence**, and a **decision**, usually involving some payment of damages, is made.

Police officers are employed by a city to uphold justice. **Sheriffs** work for the county, often functioning as "the police" in unincorporated areas that have no police force. The **Highway Patrol** are state peace officers who protect our vast highway system. **State Police** protect state buildings and officials. A **Marshal** is a county peace officer serving our court system, guarding courtrooms, serving court papers, and evicting tenants if ordered by the court.

Citizens participate directly in the justice system by serving as witnesses and on juries. In civil and criminal trials this consists of up

to twelve men and women charged with rendering a verdict. A **Grand Jury** consists of 19 citizens (23 in Los Angeles because of its large population). It investigates crimes and government operations and issues a final report to the county board of supervisors.

VIII. Class Discussion Questions

1. Does the governor appoint all judges?

2. How can the general public remove an unwanted judge?

3. What are the most serious types of crimes?

4. In your opinion, what types of investigations should your grand jury undertake?

5. Can you name at least four types of peace officers?

Chapter 9

County and City Governments

Chapter Outline

Figure 9-1

CALIFORNIA
Counties

Del Norte · Siskiyou · Modoc · Trinity · Shasta · Lassen · Humboldt · Tehama · Plumas · Mendocino · Glenn · Butte · Sierra · Nevada · Lake · Colusa · Yuba · Placer · Sutter · Yolo · El Dorado · Sonoma · Napa · Solano · Sacramento · Amador · Alpine · Marin · Calaveras · Contra Costa · San Joaquin · Tuolumne · Mono · San Francisco · Alameda · Stanislaus · Mariposa · San Mateo · Santa Clara · Merced · Madera · Santa Cruz · San Benito · Fresno · Inyo · Monterey · Tulare · Kings · San Luis Obispo · Kern · San Bernardino · Santa Barbara · Ventura · Los Angeles · Riverside · Orange · San Diego · Imperial

www.csac.counties.org (Endorsement not Implied)

I. Counties

The creation of county government in California is contained in the California Constitution and the California Government Code. A *COUNTY is the largest political subdivision of the state having corporate powers.* The Legislature vests counties with the powers necessary to provide for the needed health and welfare of the people within its borders. The specific organizational structure of a county in California will vary from county to county.

Among the distinctions between a county and a city is the fact that counties lack broad powers of self-government (e.g., cities have broad revenue generating authority and counties do not). Also, legislative control over counties is more complete than it is over cities. Unless restricted by a specific provision of the state constitution, the legislature may delegate to the counties any of the functions which belong to the state itself. Conversely, the state may take back to itself and resume the functions which it has delegated to counties (e.g., state funding of trial courts).

California State Association of Counties
www.counties.org/county-structure

There are 58 counties in California (see **Figure 9-1**). The original boundaries of the 27 counties have been split and redrawn over the years to the present 58 counties. The counties in California vary widely in size, political makeup, and geography.

A. TYPES OF COUNTIES

COUNTIES are large geographic areas initially established to bridge the gap between city governments and the state by providing services. Counties are political subdivisions of the state and their powers, duties, and obligations are set by the state legislature. The county oversees many important services, such as providing health and human services, police and fire departments, courts, roads, and park services.

The first California Constitution in 1849 provided initially for the creation of 27 counties and for the election of a board of supervisors in each county. In the early years, the county was simply an extension of the legislature and was under its direct control. The Constitutional Revision of 1879 made the functions of counties similar throughout the state, thereby bringing into existence what are known as general law

California Counties

Alameda*	Kings	Placer*	Sierra
Alpine	Lake	Plumas	Siskiyou
Amador	Lassen*	Riverside	Solano
Butte*	Los Angeles*	Sacramento*	Sonoma
Calaveras	Madera	San Benito	Stanislaus
Colusa	Marin	San	Sutter
Contra Costa	Mariposa	Bernardino*	Tehama*
Del Norte	Mendocino	San Diego	Trinity
El Dorado*	Merced	San	Tulare
Fresno*	Modoc	Francisco*	Tuolumne
Glenn	Mono	San Joaquin	Ventura
Humboldt	Monterey	San Luis Obispo	Yolo
Imperial	Napa	San Mateo*	Yuba
Inyo	Nevada	Santa Barbara	
Kern	Orange*	Santa Clara*	
		Santa Cruz	
		Shasta	

*Charter Counties

counties. *GENERAL LAW COUNTIES are counties that may establish the number of county officials and their duties, but must have the approval of the state legislature.*

In 1911 the state legislature adopted the Home Rule Amendment which allowed for the creation of charter counties. *CHARTER (HOME RULE) COUNTIES have their own charter (constitution) that allows more flexibility in collecting revenue-producing taxes, electing and appointing officials, and, in general, running and controlling the programs of the county. HOME RULE (local control) is the concept that local people are more familiar with, and therefore can solve, their problems better than some distant government body.* A charter may be adopted, amended, or repealed with majority vote approval. A new charter or the amendment or repeal of an existing charter may be proposed by the board of supervisors, a charter commission, or an initiative petition.

A charter does not give county officials extra authority over local regulations, revenue-raising abilities, budgetary decisions, or intergovernmental relations.

B. COUNTY BOARD OF SUPERVISORS

The *COUNTY BOARD OF SUPERVISORS is the county elected governing body, required by the legislature, that sets policy and budgets funds.* Most county boards consist of five members (San Francisco has eleven) who are elected in nonpartisan elections for staggered, four-year terms.

1. Women Now Run L.A. County

Voters have selected women to take charge at the L.A. County Board of Supervisors. There are four women and one man that make up the L.A. Board of Supervisors. They are:

1. Sheila Kuehl,
2. Hilda Solisa,
3. Janice Hahn,
4. Kathryn Barger, and
5. Mark Ridley-Thomas.

The Los Angeles County Board of Supervisors now can be seen as four queens and a king—they used to be called the Five Little Kings.

For many years, the board was known as the "Five Little Kings," because all five of the members were men. Terms limits have changed the composition of the Board of Supervisors. Together, they serve millions in their districts, and each has in the past helped appropriate a great deal of federal funds into L.A. County for community services.

Will the board's gender super-majority make changes in how it legislates or relates to constituents?

Each serves under newly implemented term limits of three consecutive four-year terms, diminishing a supervisor's long-term power. But will the gender super-majority make changes in how the board works together, legislates, or relates to constituents?

Historian and author Nancy Cohen's research shows "elected women tend to be more collaborative, more inclusive and more transparent" in governing.

C. COUNTY REVENUE AND EXPENSES

COUNTY REVENUE is the money that the county receives from all sources. COUNTY EXPENSES are the monies that are spent by a county to operate. The money is disbursed in the form of a budget. In Los Angeles County, for example, the estimated revenue and expense sources (best available details) are shown in **Figures 9-2** and **9-3**.

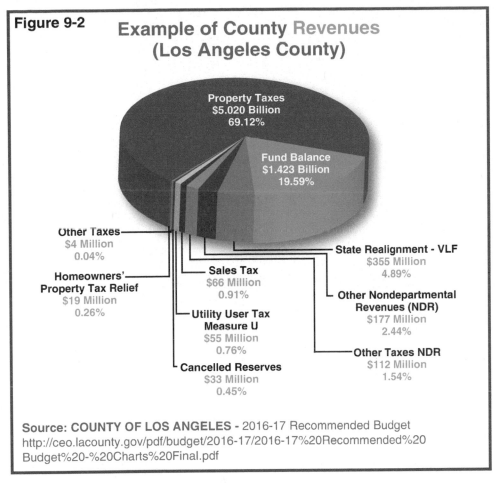

Figure 9-2

Example of County Revenues (Los Angeles County)

Property Taxes
$5.020 Billion
69.12%

Fund Balance
$1.423 Billion
19.59%

Other Taxes
$4 Million
0.04%

State Realignment - VLF
$355 Million
4.89%

Homeowners'
Property Tax Relief
$19 Million
0.26%

Sales Tax
$66 Million
0.91%

Other Nondepartmental
Revenues (NDR)
$177 Million
2.44%

Utility User Tax
Measure U
$55 Million
0.76%

Cancelled Reserves
$33 Million
0.45%

Other Taxes NDR
$112 Million
1.54%

Source: **COUNTY OF LOS ANGELES -** 2016-17 Recommended Budget
http://ceo.lacounty.gov/pdf/budget/2016-17/2016-17%20Recommended%20
Budget%20-%20Charts%20Final.pdf

Note that public protection (law enforcement), health care, public assistance, government offices, and roads and facilities account for almost the entire county expense budget, leaving little available for other needed services.

State and federal governments contribute 47% toward the budgets of the counties but also require the counties to pay out large sums for the poor through health and human services programs.

D. PROPOSITION 13 (Property Tax Limitation)

The fate of our California counties was sealed in 1978 with the passage of Proposition 13 (the Jarvis-Gann Property Tax Initiative). Proposition 13 was a direct result of businessman **Howard Jarvis** and his wife collecting tens of thousands of signatures to enable the proposition to appear on a

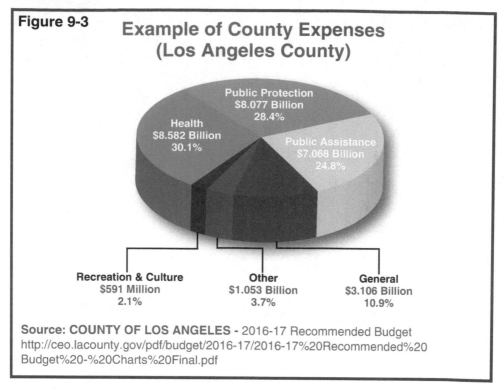

Figure 9-3

Example of County Expenses
(Los Angeles County)

Public Protection
$8.077 Billion
28.4%

Health
$8.582 Billion
30.1%

Public Assistance
$7.068 Billion
24.8%

Recreation & Culture
$591 Million
2.1%

Other
$1.053 Billion
3.7%

General
$3.106 Billion
10.9%

Source: COUNTY OF LOS ANGELES - 2016-17 Recommended Budget
http://ceo.lacounty.gov/pdf/budget/2016-17/2016-17%20Recommended%20
Budget%20-%20Charts%20Final.pdf

statewide ballot. This law set limits on the once major source of revenue for counties—property taxes.

PROPOSITION 13 *limits the amount of annual property taxes to a maximum of 1% of the March 1, 1975, market value or selling price of the property, whichever is higher, plus the cumulative increase of 2% each year thereafter.*

Before Proposition 13, if the county had a budget shortage, the county would simply increase the property tax rate and pass the entire costs on to the taxpayer. With real estate values soaring, citizens watched their tax bills soar. Angry homeowners overwhelmingly voted in support of Proposition 13 and still love it.

As a result of Proposition 13, county governments saw a massive loss in revenue amounting to billions of dollars each year. Property taxes were initially reduced to one percent from as high as four percent. The state had to pour large amounts of money into the counties, cities, school districts, etc., just to cover some of the loss. Thus, a great deal of the policy-making function shifted more powers to the legislature in Sacramento.

E. OTHER COUNTY OFFICIALS

1. Chief Administrative Officer
2. District Attorney and Public Defender
3. Assessor and Treasurer
4. Sheriff

F. FUNCTIONS OF THE COUNTY

Whether under the laws of the state in general law counties, or the guidelines of the charter in home rule counties, each county has certain duties and responsibilities that must be performed. **Many of these functions are delegated to the board of supervisors, who are responsible for their implementation and continuous supervision.** Some of the more important county functions are:

1. **Education** – County Superintendent of Schools is responsible for the overall administration and distribution of funds to schools (K-12 and community college).

2. **Law enforcement and protection of property** – The County Sheriff is responsible for the areas in the county outside of larger cities, which generally have their own police departments.

3. **Local Agency Formation Commission (LAFCO)** – A county board of supervisor's-created body whose function is to determine the boundaries of any proposed incorporated city within that county's area.

4. **Bridges and highways** – It is a county's responsibility to maintain the roads that lead into the main highways.

5. **Recreation** – each county maintains county parks.

6. **General government** – The county budget gets its share from the collection of property taxes by the County Tax Collector, and a portion of the sales tax.

G. COUNTIES LACK EXECUTIVE MANAGEMENT

One of the biggest shortcomings of county government is the inability of the public to hold one individual accountable for the condition of county government.

Each county has at least five supervisors acting as its governing body, making it impossible to single out any individual as being responsible for action or inaction. The state may have a twelve person plural executive, but the responsibility rests with the governor. Some counties

have experimented with a chief administrative officer, appointed by the board of supervisors to carry out its programs. Even with this position, **most citizens are still lost when it comes to understanding who is responsible for county government.**

II. Cities

A. A CITY IS CREATED BY INCORPORATION

In 1883, the California State Legislature adopted the Municipal Corporations Act, which classified cities according to population, and laid the groundwork for future incorporation of cities. *INCORPORATION is the process of legally forming a municipal corporation.* When referring to an incorporated area, one is talking about a city. An *UNINCORPORATED AREA is a part of a county that is not a city.*

To incorporate, a community must petition the County Board of Supervisors. The Local Agency Formation Commission (LAFCO) then holds hearings at which time the boundaries of the proposed city are set. A *LOCAL AGENCY FORMATION COMMISSION is the group that defines the exact boundary lines of cities and counties.* After approval by the LAFCO, an election is then called.

Before Proposition 13, homeowners in cities found themselves taxed twice by paying property taxes to both the county and city. Since the passage of Proposition 13, the city property tax is subtracted from the county property tax. Because of this, there is no longer any reason, for most areas, not to incorporate.

Counties exercise the powers of cities in unincorporated areas.

B. GENERAL LAW CITIES

All newly incorporated cities must begin their existence as general law cities. A *GENERAL LAW CITY has powers defined by the state's Government Code and government functions are administered by a five-member city council, elected for four-year terms.* A city clerk and treasurer are also elected for four-year terms. Other officials are appointed by the council. The mayor is chosen from the council. Some cities have a city manager or chief administrator appointed by the city council to carry out its programs. This person holds office only as long as the council desires.

Once formed, general law cities have authority to structure and manage their own affairs.

C. CHARTER (HOME RULE) CITIES

After a city becomes a general law city, it may frame a charter of its own, much like a county, and become a charter city. A *CHARTER CITY frames its own charter, enabling its citizens to better deal with current problems.*

The main advantage of a charter city is its increased power with regard to local control and government function. A charter city can exceed the tax rate that is imposed on general law cities. It can perform any municipal functions that do not violate state or national laws. Most importantly, it allows the people of the city to adjust their government to meet any special needs. Charter cities may have increased powers, but adoption and amendment of city charters requires a popular vote.

Most cities with populations over 100,000 in California are charter cities.

D. MAYOR-COUNCIL VS. COUNCIL-MANAGER

In a *MAYOR-COUNCIL type of city government*, a *MAYOR is the chief executive officer of the city*, elected by the voters, and the CITY COUNCIL *is usually a five to fifteen member nonpartisan board that is elected to handle the executive business of the city*. A *STRONG MAYOR SYSTEM usually allows the mayor some veto power over the council and power to appoint and remove certain city officials*. The best example of a strong mayor system in California is the city of San Francisco. A *WEAK MAYOR SYSTEM is one in which the office of mayor is more of a ceremonial position, with the mayor being selected from among the city council members.*

In a *COUNCIL-MANAGER form of city government, the people elect a city council and a mayor*. This is the most popular form of city government in California. The duties of the mayor are mostly ceremonial in nature. The council appoints a city manager to conduct the business of the city. A *CITY MANAGER is a professional manager who implements the city council's programs*. Over the years, the shift has been from an engineering background for a city manager toward a financial or accounting background.

E. OTHER CITY ADMINISTRATORS

1. City attorneys (prosecutors/public defenders)
2. City clerk
3. Police chief
4. Fire chief
5. Fiscal officials

Sanctuary Cities

Over 2.7 million illegal immigrants live in California- more than any other state.

There are over 200 "sanctuary cities" in 32 states that give safe harbor to illegal immigrants. **SANCTUARY CITY** *is a term that is applied by some to cities in the United States that have policies designed to not hold in custody undocumented immigrants.*

Eighteen counties and nearly 40 cities in California have policies, laws, executive orders, or regulations allowing them to avoid cooperating with federal immigration law enforcement authorities. These "sanctuary cities" ignore federal law authorizing U.S. Immigration and Customs Enforcement (ICE) to administratively deport illegal aliens without seeking criminal warrants or convictions from federal, state, or local courts." The policy is largely symbolic. City officials don't have the power to outright stop the federal government from deporting illegal immigrants in their community.

If the act is purely symbolic, however, the money issue is not. Many so-called "sanctuary cities" are putting aside funds to cover court costs of defending their sanctuary city status. **However, when many cities are "broke" or on the verge of bankruptcy, it raises the question of the fiscal responsibility of setting aside millions of dollars to protect those here illegally**.

The majority of California's undocumented immigrants are Hispanic, followed by Asians.

Can California find a balance between the financial burden of fighting the federal government to help millions of people who contribute to the state on so many levels? Will the state have to bend to the will of federal law and make the tough choice of deporting millions of productive workers and students?

The fight in California for "Sanctuary Cities" has essentially come five years too late, as a similar case was tried in Arizona and went all the way to the U.S. Supreme Court—where it was determined that the state cannot preempt federal control of immigration policy.

Sanctuary Campuses

When interviewing college instructors for this textbook, many claimed their students were expressing deep concerns about their future under Trump's administration. Since 2012, over 800,000 young people have signed up for the costly Deferred Action for Childhood Arrivals (DACA), which was implemented by President Obama. It was meant to protect undocumented immigrants who were brought to the US as children and have grown up here. It allowed them to attend school, obtain driver's licenses and in some cases, work permits.

DEFERRED ACTION FOR CHILDHOOD ARRIVALS (DACA) *is an American immigration policy that allows certain undocumented immigrants who entered the country before their 16th birthday and before June 2007 to receive a renewable two-year work permit and exemption from deportation.* DACA does confer non-immigrant legal status but does not provide a path to citizenship.

In order to protect their students, numerous college campuses are following many city examples and are declaring themselves "sanctuary campuses" who will defy authorities if asked to reveal their students' immigration status. While their intentions may be good, they may be creating a false sense of security for the students they intend to protect.

In Southern California, which is close to the Mexican border, many students are expressing tremendous fear and anxiety about their future under President Trump's administration.

Will they be allowed to stay here and continue their education? What about financial aid or getting a job after graduation?

With the state on the verge of insolvency, does supporting students who are technically here illegally make financial sense?

Can we afford to lose the educated minds of college youth or the federal funds which may be withheld from us if we don't "toe the line"?

6. Planning and community development officials
7. Public works officials
8. Recreation, parks, and community services officials
9. Librarians

F. HOW CITIES ACQUIRE AND SPEND THEIR MONEY

A city acquires most of its funds from fees and activities that occur or are generated within the city. **Figures 9-4** and **9-5** show the projected revenues and expenses for the City of San Diego.

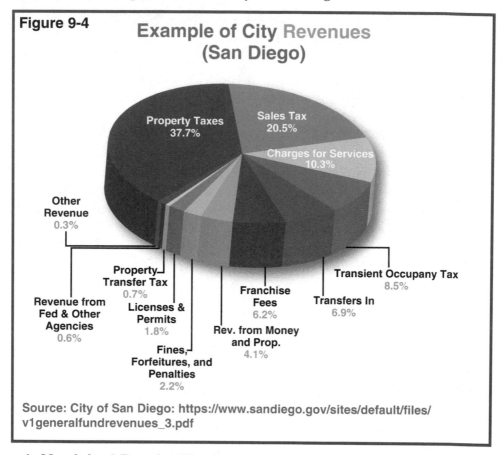

Figure 9-4

Example of City Revenues (San Diego)

Source: City of San Diego: https://www.sandiego.gov/sites/default/files/v1generalfundrevenues_3.pdf

1. Municipal Bonds: The Backbone of California Finance

Whenever California municipalities (cities, counties, etc.) need money they don't have now, they can borrow it by issuing municipal bonds—which is the equivalent to a 10- to 30-year loan. These loans are tax-free, as investors do not pay interest.

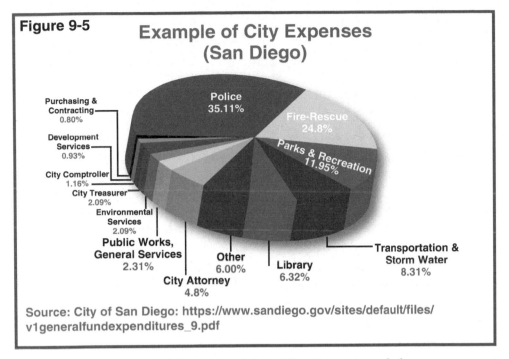

Figure 9-5

Example of City Expenses (San Diego)

Police 35.11%

Fire-Rescue 24.8%

Parks & Recreation 11.95%

Purchasing & Contracting 0.80%

Development Services 0.93%

City Comptroller 1.16%

City Treasurer 2.09%

Environmental Services 2.09%

Public Works, General Services 2.31%

City Attorney 4.8%

Other 6.00%

Library 6.32%

Transportation & Storm Water 8.31%

Source: City of San Diego: https://www.sandiego.gov/sites/default/files/ v1generalfundexpenditures_9.pdf

MUNICIPAL BONDS are debt obligations issued by government municipalities or their agencies. Examples include cities, states, and public utilities. The bond (debt) obligations are used to raise money to fund the building of schools, parks, highways, and other projects for public use.

Most municipal bonds offer income that is exempt from both federal and state taxes. Municipal bonds typically have low relative yields (interest); the interest received by a bond investor is often lower in relation to other bond types, such as corporate bonds. In effect, wealthy investors do not have to pay federal income taxes of up to around 40% and California income taxes of 11%, essentially saving 51% on the interest of the safer municipal bonds. This is great for the very wealthy who are in the highest income tax brackets, seniors and people needing less risky investments, yet looking to make a reliably reasonable interest income return their loan (municipal bonds).

The tax-free status of municipal bonds can create a tax-equivalent yield (interest) that is higher than other corporate bond types, if the city's credit rating is high. If the rate is too low, the city must pay the wealthy investors much higher interest rates.

Employers Face Tough New Standards

On January 1, 2016, SB 358, also known as **California's Fair Pay Act**, went into effect. SB 358 significantly amends **California's Equal Pay Act**, which has been codified in Labor Code section 1197.5 since 1949.

The Act amends the Labor Code in four significant ways:

1. **Employees must be paid equal wages if they perform "substantially similar work,"** meaning the employee can have a different job title and work in a different company location (i.e., a different city). Previously, the law mandated equal wages for employees performing equal work in the **same establishment**.

2. **The Act increases the burden on employers that attribute pay differences to factors other than sex.** The Act adds the requirement that an employer show that each factor is applied reasonably, and that the factors account for the entire wage differential. The Act also imposes a new analysis of a "bona fide factor other than sex."

3. The Act prohibits employers from discriminating or retaliating against employees who inquire about or discuss other employees' wages.

4. The Act extends the record-keeping requirement for wage information from two to three years.

Another Point of View

So will this new law lead to more litigation? Possibly, for these reasons:

1. Vague standards lead to more litigation. Quite simply, there's more to argue about.

2. Normally, an employee plaintiff bears the burden of proof. Yet the Fair Pay Act puts much of the burden of proof on employer defendants. When employees don't have the burden of proof, it's much easier for them to get into court and stay there.

The law provides for double damages (the wage disparity plus an equal amount for liquidated damages) plus attorneys' fees.

Public Employee Pensions
are a Ticking Time Bomb

In his State of the City speech, Los Angeles Mayor Eric Garcetti neglected to mention the more than $1.1 billion needed to pay for city employees' pensions and health care after they retire. The cost of retiree benefits amounts to nearly 20% of the city's general fund, which pays for basic city services. In 2002, the figure was less than 5%. "Every municipal government is feeling this pain," said Joe Nation, a former Democratic state legislator who teaches at Stanford University's Institute for Economic Policy Research.

An overwhelming problem seemingly misunderstood by the public is that the state and municipal public employee pension plans are fundamentally flawed, that some say operate like Ponzi Schemes, and may be similarly doomed!

A ***PONZI SCHEME*** *is a fraudulent operation that pays returns to its investors from their own money or the money paid by subsequent investors. It usually entices new investors by offering higher returns than other investments, but it requires an ever-increasing flow of money from new investors to keep the scheme going.*

Government employees' pensions are viewed by many as inherently flawed, and unable to survive without ***drastic*** fundamental reform. That is because many pension funds are dangerously underfunded to the extent that their assets are unable to meet future liabilities without either large investment returns or huge cash infusions which may be politically impossible. The debate over the size of (state, county, city and school district) pension debt tilts toward economists who "believe that the true size of the total unfunded liability debt lies closer to the larger estimates than it does to the smaller."

The pension crisis is very real. If nothing is done, our state's teachers, policemen, sanitation workers and firemen, not to mention civil service employees and others, will see their promised pensions shrink substantially. Not only will this destroy retirement nest eggs for millions of people, it will tear the social contract-pitting young against old and taxpayers against public union employees.

Reforms to date are not structural and have had little or no impact on the ever-growing unfunded liability. ▼

MAGNITUDE OF THE UNFUNDED PENSION CRISIS

Current state and municipal defined benefit pension systems are doomed because human and economic flaws guarantee they will run out of money—some sooner, some later, but all plans will run out of money eventually, unless fundamental reforms are made quickly.

Many states and municipalities will have to cut essential services, and impose a greater financial burden on citizens. A possibility exists that some plans will run out of money and governments will default on their obligations to retirees. **They have compared pension systems to "Ponzi" schemes.**

INHERENT SYSTEMIC FLAWS

Compounding the catastrophic magnitude of the pension funding crisis is the fact that the structure of public pensions locks them into a downward spiral. For example, pension funds increased their allocation to riskier investment strategies in order to maintain high discount rates and present lower liabilities. As a result, the pension funds do not behave prudently in how they manage and disclose the financing of pension systems. Risky behavior is camouflaged.

Pension reform and increased transparency are called for now. All pension plans must set the funding goal at 100 percent to avoid the potential that the current cost of pension benefits may need to be paid by future stakeholders.

FALSE SOLUTIONS

Forty-four states recently passed some type of public pension reform, but the "reforms" are widely criticized as inadequate and ineffective, because they apply only to 1) NEW employees and 2) not to current employees and 3) retirees. As a result, the reforms passed thus far have done very little, if anything, to address the ever growing unfunded liability.

With many cities nearly insolvent or bankrupt, the next generation of retirees may find only empty promises in place of their pensions.

a. Two Varieties - General Bonds and Revenue Bonds

GENERAL OBLIGATION BONDS, issued to raise immediate capital to cover expenses, are supported by the taxing power of the issuer (city or school district). REVENUE BONDS, which are issued to fund infrastructure projects, are supported by the income generated by those projects. Both types of bonds are tax exempt and particularly attractive to risk-averse investors due to the high likelihood that the issuers will repay their debts.

Glendale Community College, for example, used a general obligation bond to finance the building of a four-story parking structure, so students wouldn't have walk so far.

If the structure had financed with revenue bonds, only the students parking fees only would pay for the structure and if the students didn't pay enough money the bonds would go into bankruptcy.

b. Risk Factors

Investors buying municipal bonds may be viewed as a conservative investment strategy, but it is not risk-free.

If a bond issuer (city) is unable to meets its financial obligations, it may fail to make scheduled interest payments and/or be unable to repay the principal upon maturity. To assist in the evaluation of an issuer's creditworthiness, ratings agencies (such as Moody's Investors Service and Standard & Poor's), analyze a bond issuer's ability to meet its debt obligations.

The lower the city's rating, the higher the interest rates become, sometimes so dramatically that much-needed services or projects are eliminated or postponed.

G. COUNTIES BILL CITIES FOR SERVICES

Proposition 13 fixed property tax rates initially at 1% of the purchase price. As a result, counties rely more upon an increased revenues from sales taxes for their funding. The counties now have an incentive to increase sources of sales taxes by, among other things, permitting more strip, auto, and regional malls, or "Big Box Stores," like Walmart.

Since commercial properties bring in sales taxes, which residential properties do not, there is no incentive given to counties and cities to permit zoning for affordable residential housing for the middle class and poor.

The state legislature allowed our under-funded counties to charge the cities within their county a "prisoner booking fee" and "property tax collection fee." This greatly concerns our California cities because they see this as the first in a series of steps that could mandate programs in the county for which the cities would be charged.

The city government provides the following services:

1. **Protective services** – Includes law enforcement, fire protection and civil defense. The highest percentage of funds is spent on these items.

2. **Recreation, health, education** – This includes parks and playgrounds. Health services are often in conjunction with county programs. Schools are run and maintained through school districts.

3. **Public works** – Improvement and maintenance of city streets, off-street parking, collection of trash and sanitation.

4. **General government** – Most cities utilize the county tax facilities to collect tax money.

III. Districts

A. DISTRICT FUNCTIONS

DISTRICTS are geographic units designated for a specific governmental purpose, usually to provide a public service, such as mosquito abatement, flood control, and education.

Districts can co-exist with a city or county but often they do not. There are about 6,000 districts in California, of which at least 1,000 are K-12 or community college school districts.

B. CREATION OF A DISTRICT

The establishment and organization of districts is provided for by state law. In order to form a district, a petition must be signed by the voters living within the boundaries of the proposed district. This petition is presented to the board of supervisors. A majority vote is needed by the board, or in some cases the electorate, to establish a district.

C. SPECIAL DISTRICTS

A *SPECIAL DISTRICT is a form of local government created by a local community to meet a specific need.* Inadequate tax bases and competing demands for existing taxes make it hard for cities and counties to provide all the services their citizens desire. When residents or landowners want new services or higher levels of existing services, they can form a district to pay for and administer them.

Nearly 85% of California's special districts perform a single function such as sewage, water, fire protection, pest abatement, or cemetery management. Multi-function districts, like community services districts, provide two or more services (see **Figure 9-6**).

Figure 9-6

Examples of Types of Special Districts

Airport Districts
Cemetery Districts
Community Services Districts
Drainage Districts
Flood Control, Water
Conservation Districts
Fire Protection Districts
Healthcare/Hospital Districts
Harbor/Ports Districts
Improvement Districts
Irrigation Districts
Library Districts
Mosquito Abatement/Vector
  Control Districts

Park and Recreation Districts
Police Protection Districts
Reclamation Districts
Recreation & Park/Open Space
Districts
Resource Conservation
  Districts
Sanitation/Sewer Districts
Transit Districts
Utility Districts
Water Districts

Source: California Special Districts Association
http://www.csda.net/special-districts/

D. SCHOOL DISTRICTS

The largest category of districts in California is the school districts.

There are over 1,000 school districts in California. Every segment of California is divided into school districts. School districts include: elementary, high school, unified (K-12), union (high school district that encompasses several elementary districts), and community college.

Each school district has a board of education. The board of education generally consists of five members chosen in a nonpartisan election held within each district. The board has the responsibility of hiring principals and teachers (or presidents and professors at community colleges), and all support staff for the district. It also adopts the school budgets and determines the curriculum.

Each board is accountable to the State Board of Education, the ten member board appointed by the governor and administered by the state Superintendent of Public Instruction. Each community college board of trustees has individual power to govern its own district. It is overseen by the state board of governors of the 113 community colleges, serving over 2.1 million students.

www.cde.ca.gov (Department of Education)
www.mwdh2o.com/ (Metropolitan Water District - MWD)

E. WATER DISTRICTS

The *METROPOLITAN WATER DISTRICT (MWD) was organized to provide Southern California with water to supplement its dwindling water supply.*

Running along the Pacific Ocean from Oxnard to the Mexican border and inland for 70 miles, the MWD boundaries extend into six counties: San Diego, San Bernardino, Riverside, Orange, Los Angeles, and Ventura. The MWD supplies about half of the water used within its service area and is expected to handle nearly all of the anticipated increases in the future. Of course, the amount of water supplied will depend on deliveries from the California Aqueduct and the Colorado River Aqueduct.

IV. Regional Governance

A. TREND FROM COUNTY TO REGIONAL DISTRICTS

The dramatic growth of Los Angeles, Ventura, Orange, Riverside, and San Bernardino counties has created a mostly urban area where the boundaries of counties and cities are so close together that they are hard to distinguish.

A *REGION is a large geographic unit that can include many cities and counties and cover a large portion of a state.* The common problems of cities and counties have led to the idea of regional governance.

REGIONAL GOVERNANCE is the process of regional planning and policy making with the help of cities, counties, and businesses within the region. Water shortages, air pollution, and transportation are just some of the issues which cross city or county lines and might be handled more efficiently at the regional level. When counties or cities are overwhelmed by a problem and underwhelmed by the resources needed to handle it, a regional approach seems to be the best answer.

Regional financing is the new way to solve regional problems. Los Angeles county is now collecting an additional half-cent sales tax to help solve transportation problems by linking together transit lines from many cities within the county. The Metropolitan Water District helps furnish most of the water for Southern California and bills according to usage. This trend will continue with regard to our air quality and waste management.

B. COUNCILS OF GOVERNMENT (COGs)

A *COUNCIL OF GOVERNMENT (COG) is an association of city and county government officials, within a given region, whose purpose is to find solutions to common problems.* These COGs help solve common area problems quickly and cooperatively while maintaining the home rule style of government.

 The **Southern California Association of Governments (SCAG)** (www.scag.ca.gov) and the **Association of Bay Area Governments (ABAG)** (www.abag.ca.gov) are California's two major COGs.

ABAG has been successful in making regional plans for such important matters as transportation, refuse disposal, recreational facilities, and shoreline development. The SCAG is the largest COG in the United States, serving over 13 million people in a 38,000 square mile area. SCAG has been successful in coordinating the planned connection between the Southern California Rapid Transit District (SCRTD) and the Orange County Transit District (OCTD).

Most of California's regional problems are not being financed or solved by the federal or state government. Clean air and pollution standards by the *AIR QUALITY MANAGEMENT DISTRICT (AQMD) have been made strict to reduce air pollution for the region.* Federal standards, although well meaning, do not take into account Southern California's unique air pollution problems. So, basically, the federal government has complicated matters rather than offered viable solutions. Frankly, the state and federal governments have given Southern California mandates regarding air pollution but have not given the area the funds with which to accomplish these mandates. *MANDATES are the requirements for programs implemented by the state or federal government.*

V. Chapter Summary

Our California city and county governments face great challenges. Greater demands are being placed on them than ever before, but local government lacks the definitive political clout necessary to effectively administer these services.

Counties are large geographical areas that bridge the gap between cities and the state by providing services at the local level. The California Constitution created the original 27 counties. **There are now 58.** The original counties were considered **general law counties,** and functioned only under the close supervision of the state legislature. Later, under the **Home Rule Amendment of 1911,** counties were permitted to designate themselves as **charter (or home rule)** counties, permitting more autonomy to set policy and collect taxes.

A county government is administered by the **County Board of Supervisors,** usually five members elected to four-year terms. They decide public policy, budget funds, and make various local appointments. County governments are primarily responsible for several important public functions: education, law enforcement, define city and county boundaries, **Local Agency Formation Commission (LAFCO),** maintenance of bridges and highways, recreation, and taxes.

County revenue also comes from the state, the federal government, fund balance sources, property taxes, sales taxes, and other fees. These state and federal contributions are not without strings attached, and most of the money they give the counties is passed on directly to the public as health and human services programs.

In 1978, **Proposition 13** passed, limiting the amount of property taxes that could be collected by the county. Local governments saw a loss in revenue and the state had to fill the void, pouring millions of dollars into the counties to keep their schools, law enforcement, recreation, and other necessary programs operating. But with each dollar came more state control.

Counties, on average, spend most of their budgets on public protection, health, and public assistance. Very little is left for other areas such as education, recreation and culture, debt service, and reserves.

Cities are created by **incorporating**, a process that is similar to forming a business corporation. They are formed from unincorporated areas of the county or split from other cities with the proper voters' approval. All cities start as **general law cities** but most become **charter (home rule) cities** when their population grows and they want less state regulation.

In a **council-manager** form of city government, which is the most common in California, the city is run by a professional city manager.

In the **mayor-council** form of city government, the mayor and council direct the different agencies that run the city. These cities are governed by a nonpartisan elected board of 5 to 15 members, called a city council, and a mayor, who is selected to lead this group. Either the mayor is elected by the city council or is elected separately by the voters. If the mayor comes from a **weak mayor system**, the duties are mostly ceremonial. In a **strong mayor system**, the mayor can make appointments and remove certain city officials.

Although cities vary greatly, most cities collect their money from these sources: 1) real property taxes, 2) sales taxes, and 3) charges for services. Cities spend their money mostly on: 1) police, 2) fire-rescue, and 3) parks and recreation.

There are about 6,000 districts in California. **Districts** are geographical units designed for a specific governmental purpose, such as flood control, mosquito abatement, or for schools. Perhaps one of the best known districts is the **Metropolitan Water District (MWD).**

There are more than 1,000 K-12 school districts. There are 72 districts and 113 colleges, enrolling more than 2.9 million students, that comprise the California Community College System. **Community colleges** provide basic skills education, real estate education, workforce training, and courses that prepare students for transfer to four-year universities. Opportunities for personal enrichment and lifelong learning are offered. Tuition has gone from $26 to $46 a unit under the Brown Administration in a little over a year. The Community College students sense that they are carrying more than their fair share of the state's financial burden.

Regional governance may take the place of a local government on certain issues in the future because many of California's problems cross over city and county lines.

VI. Class Discussion Questions

1. What made the formation of California cities so popular?

2. What does California's Fair Pay Act do?

3. What are the differences between California cities using either a weak or strong mayoral system?

4. What are the pros and cons of amending Proposition 13?

5. What are the strong and weak points of (county, city, district, and regional) governmental units in California?

Chapter 10

Our State Budget Crisis

I. California's Ongoing State Budget Crisis

www.dof.ca.gov (Department of Finance)
www.ebudget.ca.gov (California Budget)

The California state budget crisis is due in part to our slowing population growth. Our budget is constantly on the verge of a deficit crisis and income taxes and regulations are at an all time high. California's schools and jails are crowded, highways are congested, roads are deteriorating rapidly, and more than 20.6% of the population is living at or below the poverty level—and that number continues to grow. The system cannot keep up.

Some say that all we need to continue our road to recovery is maintain our high level of state erratic income taxation and create new laws and regulations. This is not a realistic approach to take. All taxes are very high and, if they are increased, even more businesses will leave the state, taking needed jobs and growth with them. **Californians are already among the highest taxed people in the United States**.

The solution may be to operate our state government more like a business.

With some good leadership from state and local politicians, the problems facing California can be addressed.

215

Chapter Outline

California's Population is Growing Older Daily

California's working population, known as **"earners"** is slowly increasing, but many more baby boomers have retired and more are approaching retirement every day. Unfortunately, too many earners who currently contribute the most in taxes are leaving the state when they retire, or may become "spenders" if they stay.

To make matters worse, the percentage of Californian's living below the poverty level, known as **"users,"** is an eye-popping 20.6 percent—the highest in the nation. This group is least likely to help increase California's tax revenues.

We are continuing to see moderate population growth, mostly because of the high cost of renting or buying a home. The following is a breakdown of the three population groups in California:

1. **Earners** (Age 18 to 64) – Working population is slowly growing
2. **Spenders** (65 and older) – Social security and pensioners
3. **Users** (Mostly under 18 or on welfare) – Receiving public services: education, child care, human services, and public health care.

"Earners" are the number of job holders (most with some college education) that have seen their incomes go up in percentage terms. Many of the large group of baby boomers (born 1946 to 1964) have retired and soon many more will also be leaving the workforce.

Older Californians (**"spenders"**) are increasing in number, to about 14% of the state's population. The number of Californians 65 years of age and older will continue growing annually at around 4% for years to come. Nearly half are expected to move from the suburbs to a more convenient city type of living. These **"spenders"** are positive contributors to the economy because they spend money and pay more than their fair share in state income and sales taxes. Unfortunately, over one million well-to-do seniors have moved out of our state in the last decade.

The **"users"** group are younger (or families on welfare) and use California's public service tax dollars in the form of education, child care, human services, and public health care. The huge growth within this group is due to slightly higher birthrates among our immigrant population. The end result of these demographic groups is that they drive up state and local government expenses, while at the same time reducing the revenue generated by state income taxes and sales taxes.

California's Older Seniors: In Crisis

California's over 65 years of age population is expected to grow from 14% today to a huge 21% of the state's population by 2025. **In California, over 1,250 people will start turning 65 each day**. Seniors will remain a large percentage of the population over the next two decades because of: 1) a longer life expectancy, and 2) generally lower birth rates.

The big problem is that most workers are financially unprepared for retirement, with many leaving California as part of our mounting retirement crisis. The retirement crisis is national in scope, but California seniors face a much higher cost-of-living due to our high rents and home prices. This is why so many seniors are moving to places like Denver and Las Vegas. Students should save money monthly, invest, and buy a house so that their 30-year loan is paid off by retirement time.

The **"quality of life"** is the big potential crisis facing seniors. Older seniors, seniors of color, older women, unmarried seniors, and renters are likely to be poor and will struggle. **Soon, 30% of senior Californians will not be able to afford basic needs.**

The Budget Process Timeline

Governor's Proposed Budget (January)	Revision (May)	Enacted Budget (Summer)
The Budget proposed by the Governor	Changes to the Governor's Proposed Budget based on the latest economic forecasts	The Budget passed by the Legislature and signed by the Governor

Source: ebudget.ca.gov

II. The California State Budget

The *STATE GENERAL FUND BUDGET* is the state government's financial plan for spending and taxing that is proposed by the governor each year with much fanfare and passed by the legislature for each fiscal year.

Federal, state, and county governments only use a fiscal year instead of a calendar year. The *GOVERNMENTAL FISCAL YEAR* is a 365-day year that starts on July 1 and ends on June 30. For example, if the governor, mayor, or a school board member refers to the 2017-2018 fiscal year, he or she is referring to the year from July 1, 2017 to June 30, 2018.

There are no deficits allowed in state budgets. A **DEFICIT** *occurs when the current money collected from the people, in the form of taxes, is not enough to pay for the agreed-upon expenses.* The government borrows money in many different ways to make sure the general fund budget is balanced, but the huge amount owed are "off" the general fund budget and are called **"unfunded liabilities."**

A. THE BUDGET PROCESS (General Fund)

The complicated budget process stretches over an 18-month period. The budget phases, lasting six months each, are:

1. Budget construction stage: **"What do you want?"**
2. Department of Finance refinement stage: **"Be realistic."**
3. Legislative debate stage: **"Only getting what we give."**

Each January, after the governor's State of the State Address, the budget is submitted to the legislature and the public. The legislature, after debating it at length and passing it with the required two-thirds vote of both houses, submits the approved budget to the governor. The submission deadline date to the governor is June 15.

Remember: the governor has line item veto power. The **LINE ITEM VETO** *means the governor can eliminate or reduce any budget item he or she does not like.* The budget then goes back to the legislature, which has the constitutional power to override the governor's veto with a two-thirds vote in each house—they seldom succeed.

B. CALIFORNIA'S BUDGET PROBLEMS

California's demographics show the increasing number of immigrants and their children, people needing county health and welfare services, and the number of automobiles using our congested freeways.

How will California handle its growth problems in a state where the residents are already among the most (and increasingly) taxed in the country? There are several different ways for our lawmakers to reduce the budget. Reasonable solutions to our increasing population that is at or near the poverty level (20.6%) must be given priority. The budget can then be lightened by searching for new practical answers. The budget problems created by our slower population growth over the past decades are real. The question is how will we deal with all these problems at once?

III. Sources of State Revenues

A. THE FOUR MAIN TAXES

In order to understand California's basic tax structure, it is best to look at the four main sources of state taxes in detail. Who pays these taxes, and what rate they pay, are political questions. The state's taxing policy (revenue), which is implemented by our governor and legislature, changes over time (see **Figure 10-1**).

#1 – State Personal Income Taxes (68.6% of Budget)

California is a "Trillion Dollar Economy." The yearly amount of taxes will increase as will spending, but "how" is decided by our lawmakers.

The ***STATE FRANCHISE TAX BOARD (FTB) (www.ftb.ca.gov)*** *is the California state agency that collects state income taxes from individuals and corporations.* The state personal income tax is the single largest source of taxes in California. Currently, the state income tax rate went up to 13.3% for those in the highest bracket. Remember: federal income taxes, which have a top rate of 39.6%, must be paid in addition to the state income taxes. Some other states, such as Nevada, Florida, and Washington, do not even charge their citizens any personal income tax. This is another reason why some of our least and more affluent residents are tempted to leave California.

State income taxes are indexed. ***INDEXING*** *is the periodic adjustment of income tax brackets to eliminate the effects of inflation.* This means that if the inflation rate is 3% for the year, the tax bracket will also go up by 3% to compensate for the difference. The taxpayer, although making more money, may still remain in the same high tax bracket.

#2 - Sales and Use Tax (20.1% of Budget)

California's sales tax generally applies to the sale of merchandise, including vehicles, in the state. California's alternative use tax applies to the use, storage, or other consumption of those same kinds of items in the state.

Sales tax on automobiles is a large figure and divided between the state and cities where the dealerships are located. This is why many cities give auto dealers special street names and addresses.

The ***STATE BOARD OF EQUALIZATION (www.boe.ca.gov)*** *is the California state agency that collects state sales taxes from businesses which, in turn, collect sales taxes from the consumer at the point of purchase.*

Figure 10-1

California General Fund Revenue Sources
(Dollars in Millions)

Personal Income Tax	$85,866
Sales and Use Tax	25,179
Corporation Tax	10,878
Insurance Tax	2,368
Alcoholic Beverage Taxes and Fees	372
Cigarette Tax	65
Motor Vehicle Fees	24
Other	431
Subtotal	**$125,183**
Transfer to Rainy Day Fund	-1,156
Total	**$124,027**

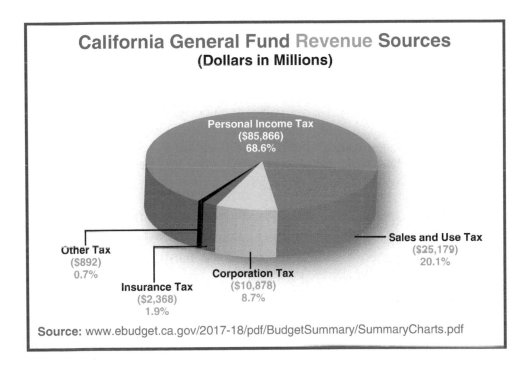

California General Fund Revenue Sources
(Dollars in Millions)

Personal Income Tax
($85,866)
68.6%

Sales and Use Tax
($25,179)
20.1%

Corporation Tax
($10,878)
8.7%

Insurance Tax
($2,368)
1.9%

Other Tax
($892)
0.7%

Source: www.ebudget.ca.gov/2017-18/pdf/BudgetSummary/SummaryCharts.pdf

California relies "too much" on personal income taxes because it goes up and down dramatically depending on the current economy.

Wholesalers do not pay sales taxes because they are not the ultimate consumer. The current sales tax base rate is 7.5%, but this base rate can be increased up to around 9.5% on an individual city or county basis, if approved by the voters.

Generally, if sales tax would apply when you buy physical merchandise in California, **use tax** applies when you make a similar purchase without tax from a business located outside the state. For these purchases, the buyer is required to pay use tax separately. Most "online purchases" add sales tax for Californians.

#3 – Corporation Tax (8.7% of Budget)

In addition to collecting income taxes on individuals, the state also collects income taxes on corporations, whose shares of stock are mostly owned by individuals, and the pension plans of most unions or businesses. The corporation tax is imposed on businesses that do business in California and derive income from within and outside California.

Over the past decade, the FTB has collected an average of $9.5 billion per year in "state" corporation income taxes. President Trump has proposed reducing "federal" corporation taxes.

#4 – Insurance Tax (1.9% of Budget)

All insurance companies are subject to tax on: 1) gross premiums, 2) "retaliatory tax" (owed when an insurance company domiciled in another state imposes higher taxes and fees on a California-domiciled insurer in the same business), and 3) gross insurance premiums on ocean marine insurers.

B. EFFECTS OF TAXES: (The Poor and the Wealthy)

Taxes do not affect all people in the same way. Certain taxes affect the poor more than the wealthy, and certain taxes hardly affect the poor, but definitely hurt the wealthy. The goal should be a tax policy that requires very little from the poor and more (but not too much) from the wealthy. Of course, the same policy would collect most of the taxes from the middle group referred to as "average" Californians.

A *REGRESSIVE TAX is a tax that is larger as a percentage of income for lower income people.* A good example of a regressive tax is the California state sales tax. This tax takes up a larger portion of the lower income individual's personal budget because almost all of his or her income is used to buy items subject to this tax. It has a big impact on people who have the least amount of money. Governor Brown's recent tax increases on gasoline **(12%)**, energy, and car registration **(42%)** are regressive, and are a larger burden on lower income groups.

A *PROGRESSIVE TAX is a tax that increases as a percentage of income as the wealth of the taxpayer increases.* The best example of a progressive tax is the California state income tax on individuals and businesses. Poor people may not pay any income taxes, middle-income Californians pay a large amount, and the wealthy pay the most, on an individual basis. This tax affects the rich the most because they are in the highest tax bracket and therefore pay the most money. Recent income tax increases on the wealthy are progressive, and encourage these people to move or invest out of state.

SIN TAXES are the taxes paid for the purchase and consumption of alcoholic beverages, tobacco products, and marijuana. These taxes have increased dramatically in recent years. The tax is not only applied to hard liquors but also to wines and beers and our newly approved recreational drug, marijuana. In 2017, the cigarette tax rose to $2.00 per pack, with equivalent increases on other tobacco products and electronic cigarettes.

Is It Time to Fix the Top-Heavy State Income Tax?

The nation's heaviest state income tax burden, by far, is carried by Californians, especially the wealthy. President Trump and the U.S. Congress could make it a lot worse if they eliminate the ability to deduct state and local taxes on federal 1040s, which is in a plan hatched by House Republicans.

California's state income tax is very high, with rates ranging from 1% to 13.3%. Oregon is the state with the second-highest rate at 9.9%. But unlike California, Oregon doesn't also impose a state sales tax.

Californians are projected to fork over roughly $83 billion in state income taxes in 2017, supplying 69% of the general fund.

California's state tax system is antiquated—the revenue stream has become unreliable because it depends too much on the capital gains of high-income earners. ▼

During a recession, capital gains go bust and the revenue slows to a trickle, creating massive budget deficits and jeopardizing vital programs such as education, health care, and public safety. As an example, during the recession in 2008, a 3.7% decline in the California economy resulted in a 23% plunge in state revenue.

There has to be a more reliable system that doesn't constantly go up and down. Perhaps the top income tax rate should be reduced a couple of points and capital gains could be taxed at a lower rate (as the feds do) and at the same time easing the sales tax rate while extending it to services, like other states.

1. Earned-Income Tax Credit Gift for Low-Wage Workers

California's has joined the federal government in giving unearned money to low-wage workers, (redistribution method) by giving additional extra money as refunds on their annual tax returns. This return of more (extra) money than they paid in is a **gift** called an **earned-income tax credit** for only low wage workers.

California's state version is in addition to the similar federal earned-income tax credit, though less generous. People who earn $13,800 or less get rebates up to thousands of dollars, depending on family size.

Almost 500,000 California workers are currently receiving this extra money back in the form of a tax credit. To qualify, they need to be employed. Lawmakers should be fair and expand the state credit to include people who are self-employed, an acknowledgment that people who go from one job to the next make up an ever-larger segment of the "gig" workforce (a *GIG describes a single project or task for which a worker is hired*). A *GIG ECONOMY is a labor market characterized by the prevalence of short-term contracts or freelance work as opposed to permanent jobs*. As artificial intelligence (disruptive technology) applications increase, the number of available jobs will be reduced even more.

C. DO GENEROUS LAWMAKERS TAX US TOO MUCH?

California's taxes will remain high in the foreseeable future because of the many problems created by our slowing population growth. Most of the badly needed solutions will require funds that the state does not possess at this time. So the challenge to lawmakers (California governor, senate, and assembly) is: How will they decide, among competing alternatives, which worthy programs will receive the most money and attention to make our state better?

IV. Expenditures: Where Taxes Go

A. THE FOUR LARGEST EXPENDITURES

The four largest expenditures represent more than 90% of the state's budget. In descending order of cost, they are: (#1) K-12 Education, (#2) Health and Human Services, and (#3) Higher Education (community colleges and state universities), and (#4) Corrections and Rehabilitation. California's economic recovery will someday provide more money in the budget for newer, more innovative programs after funding these big costly programs (see **Figures 10-2** and **10-3**).

Figure 10-2

California General Fund Expeditures (Dollars in Millions)	
K-12 Education	$52,169
Health and Human Services	33,994
Higher Education	14,627
Corrections and Rehabilitation	11,088
Other	10,642
Total	**$122,520**

#1 COST – K-12 Education (42.6% of Expenditures)

Most of California's General Fund Expenditures go to K-12 schools, community colleges, Cal State, and University of California.

More money is spent educating our students from kindergarten through high school and supporting community college students than on any other state function. K-12 and higher education represents 54.5% of the state budget. Each school or community college district is technically owned by the state but governed, controlled, and administered by a local board that is elected by the voters. *LOCAL CONTROL means that the administrators and teachers (mostly union members) are hired by the local board of education to administer and teach the subjects approved by the voter selected local board of education.*

The state provides 70% of all the educational costs to each district. About 30% of the money for schools and community colleges comes

Figure 10-3

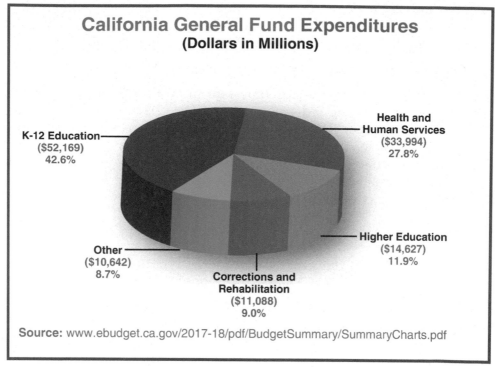

California General Fund Expenditures
(Dollars in Millions)

K-12 Education—
($52,169)
42.6%

Health and
Human Services
($33,994)
27.8%

Higher Education
($14,627)
11.9%

Corrections and
Rehabilitation
($11,088)
9.0%

Other —
($10,642)
8.7%

Source: www.ebudget.ca.gov/2017-18/pdf/BudgetSummary/SummaryCharts.pdf

Remember that a large amount of debt ("Unfunded Liabilities") in the form of pensions for teachers and public employees is hidden "off budget" (not disclosed to the public).

from the local governments that collect funds in the form of real estate property taxes. In addition, the state lottery generates about 3% of the funds.

For the 2017-2018 fiscal year, the budget provides for sufficient resources to fully fund the workload budget required by the landmark Proposition 98. Money is used to support average daily attendance costs within school districts and charter schools and Career Technical Education. For community colleges, resources will also support a cost-of-living adjustment for apportionments for enrollment growth.

It costs approximately $15,216 a year, per student, to educate a child in the K-12 public school system (see Figure 10-4).

Figure 10-4

K-12 Education Spending Per Pupil

$10,910 **(Proposition 98)**
$4,306 **(Local Sources)**
$15,216 **(Total)**

Source: www.ebudget.ca.gov/2017-18/pdf/BudgetSummary/SummaryCharts.pdf

---

TRUMP ANXIETY

Medi-Cal (what the federal program **Medicaid** is called here) is the very basic health care system in California. President Donald Trump has promised to restructure Medicaid—a move that could be acutely felt in California, where one in three residents receive health coverage through the state version.

Some of those Californians could lose portions of their benefits or possibly be dropped from coverage altogether if President Trump carries out his plan, which would likely cost the state billions. Even residents who relied on the program long before the current expansion could be affected.

President Trump and his Secretary of Health and Human Services, Tom Price, have said they want to limit spending by giving states a fixed amount of money each year. States will then have an incentive to eliminate fraud, waste, and abuse.

But the federal government contribution will probably be less than what states are currently receiving and won't increase enough over time to keep pace with rising costs, forcing states to either reallocate funds to fill the gap or make cuts.

#2 COST – Health Care and Human Services (27.8% of Expenditures)

Public health care has been constantly declining because of the lower income population increases. Providing health services to Californians who do not have health insurance is nearly impossible. The number of people who obtain free health care keeps rising. California has 12.5% of the U.S. population, but must support 16% of the nation's health care recipients. Unfortunately, each year health care services will continue to take up a larger portion of the state budget.

33% of all Californians are low-income families (adult 19-64, children, pregnant women, seniors, or disabled) on Medi-Cal (Medicaid).

TRUMP ANXIETY

President Trump's health care legislation passed the U.S. House of Representatives (with all Californian Republican members voting yes.) He will be held responsible (positively or negatively) by the general public for any resulting health care changes since he "repealed and replaced" Obamacare. No matter what changes there are to future health care legislation (Medicare and Medicaid), it will be phased in gradually over many years.

#3 COST – Higher Education (11.9% of Expenditures)

Most California community college students do not realize that it costs about $5,000 annually to educate a full-time student. Even at $46 a unit a semester for tuition and fees, they are getting one of the best college educational bargains anywhere in the United States.

A recent increase of 30% has forced students on University of California campuses to pay more for tuition. Student fees at the California State University will continue to be a bargain.

The 2017 estimated annual undergraduate tuition fees are:

1. **University of California** – California resident - $13,500; nonresident - $40,182.

2. **California State University** – California resident - $5,472; nonresident - $5,472 + $372 per semester unit.

California Community Colleges Key Facts

The California Community College system is the nation's largest system of higher education, made up of 113 colleges, 72 districts, and 2.1 million students.

Value to California:

- Twenty-nine percent of University of California and 51 percent of California State University graduates started at a California community college.

- Transfer students from the California Community Colleges to the University of California system currently account for 48 percent of UC's bachelor's degrees in science, technology, engineering and mathematics.

High Return on College Education:

- The California Community College system is the largest provider of workforce training in the state and nation.

- For every $1 California invests in students who graduate from college, it will receive a net return on investment of $4.50.

- Californians with a college degree will earn $400,000 more in their lifetime than their peers with only a high school diploma.

- Students who earn a degree or certificate from a California community college nearly double their earnings within three years.

Workforce Skills Gap:

- With baby boomers retiring as the best-educated and most skilled workforce in U.S. history, labor experts are concerned that California will lack workers with the critical aptitude needed to replace them.

Distance Education (Online) Fact Sheet:

- California community colleges lead the way in distance education.

- Of all courses offered at California's community colleges, 12.3 percent are offered through distance education, and it is estimated that nearly half of all courses have some online component.

▼

General Facts:

- With more than 2.1 million students on 113 campuses, the California Community Colleges is the largest system of higher education in the United States.

- One in every five community college students in the nation attends a California community college.

- Three out of every 10 Californians ages 18-24 are currently enrolled in a community college.

Student Demographics by Ethnicity

African-American	6.41%	Pacific Islander	0.43%
Native American	0.44%	White	27.42%
Asian	11.56%	Multi-Ethnicity	3.73%
Filipino	2.8%	Unknown	4.72%
Hispanic	42.48%		

Student Demographics by Age

≤19	25.87%
20-24	31.67%
25-29	13.92%
30-34	7.82%
35 and over	20.7%
Unknown	0.02%

Student Demographics by Gender

Female	53.31%
Male	45.54%
Unknown	1.15 %

California residents currently pay $46 per unit for community college courses. A California resident who enrolls in 12 units is considered a full-time student; that student would pay $46 x 12 units, or $552 per semester.

#4 COST – Corrections and Rehabilitation (9% of Expenditures)

The mission of the **California Department of Corrections and Rehabilitation (CDCR)** is to enhance public safety through safe and secure incarceration of the most serious and violent offenders, effective parole supervision, and rehabilitative strategies to successfully reintegrate offenders into our communities.

There are over 130,000 men and women in California prisons, more than any other state. The public's fear of crime, which is fed by the news media, demands that politicians be tough on criminals. The problem is that it costs over $64,000 a year to house a prisoner. Sadly, 70% of released prisoners are returned to prison within three years.

B. MOST SPENDING IS EARMARKED

Most state government spending is earmarked for special purposes. *EARMARKED FUNDS are those that have been committed and budgeted ahead of time to accomplish a certain purpose.* An example of earmarked funds are gas taxes, which are supposed to be used to build roads and highways, even though the state now needs more funds for "pet" mass transit systems.

C. LACK OF TRANSPARENCY IS UNETHICAL

Are state agencies unethically hiding funds or worse?

The legislature is growing more frustrated over revelations of possible civil, administrative, or even criminal violations by state agencies for hiding state funds by not depositing them in the state treasury.

A director of the state Treasurer's Office has so far identified 50 accounts by various state agencies where money was not put into the state treasury as it should have been. This has got to stop. All financial accounting information should have *TRANSPARENCY, which means transactions should properly be accounted for and stated on the financial statements.* Accounting transparency is extremely important for the general public. (See discussion of **Prop 54, Legislative Transparency**, in Chapter 7.)

D. BIG FINANCIAL PROBLEM - GENEROUS PENSIONS

We must fix to our huge hidden unfunded teachers and public employee pensions! Our "hidden" debt is close to $3 Trillion.

California's Supreme Court Bankrupt Pensions' Ruling Could Be a Shocker!

A California Supreme Court ruling could make all of us face the non-transparent unfunded pension problem that may bankrupt the state.

California needs to fix the problem now or face bankruptcy in the future. The state appellate and supreme courts must rule to only allow "reasonable pensions" to be paid, not the promised ones.

There are four things we can do that Rhode Island has already done to correct the same type of pension funding problems: 1) Correct false return percentages on pension investments, 2) Mandate that all new teachers will now receive smaller pensions, 3) Mandate that in three years all teachers will get one-half of promised pensions, and 4) Accept our Supreme Court ruling of paying "only reasonable pensions."

School districts are now taking money away from our children's education so our retired teachers can keep their pensions.

Our school districts' taxes are increasing in order to pay Governor Brown's and our legislature's underfunded pension liabilities.

In private, every knowledgeable official will tell you we are heading for insolvency because insignificant corrections are being made now.

It's not the elephant in the room, it's the pension dinosaur!

This state is on the verge of insolvency. We cannot afford to pay the huge unfunded liabilities promised to our teachers. This issue could well pit teachers unions and school districts against California taxpayers if the state must pay to correct this huge unfunded pension debt.

The latest signs show there is something financially off. The California State Teachers' Retirement System (CalSTRS) lowered its official investment forecast in a move expected to require higher contributions from state taxpayers for the teachers' pension fund. But this will still not be enough to fix the growing pension obligations. Public pension funds have been lowering their investment return forecasts in recent years. The less money they make from investment accounts, the more pension funds will be needed from taxpayers and employee contributors.

The annual contributions from school districts has grown from $2 billion to $6 billion over the last several years.

V. Bonds Mean Debt

When the state of California needs to borrow large amounts of money (too large to be borrowed from banks), we issue long-term bonds (debt). The state must sell bonds to the general public in order to raise funds. A *BOND is a debt, a loan in increments of $1,000, made to the state of California, which will be repaid by the state to the owner of the bond on a certain date, usually anywhere from 10 to 30 years.* In effect, this is an installment credit program to purchase buildings or finance construction projects. Voters must approve each bond issue. There are two types of bonds.

A *GENERAL OBLIGATION BOND is secured by everything the state owns.* It is used when the project the bond is funding will not earn enough interest money.

A *REVENUE BOND is backed up only by the revenue generated by that project or taxing district.* The state uses revenue bonds to finance dams, canals, bridges, and other projects that can generate income. Buyers of these bonds rely on credit rating agencies to analyze the creditworthiness of the issue.

President Trump has promised to invest in much needed infrastructure repair. Will California agree to help by issuing bonds (10- to 30-year debt) that will be used to finance the repair of such infrastructure as dams, highways, and ports? As bonds are a form of debt meant to be paid off over several decades, this should have a minimal effect on the current state budget.

VI. Business Climate

California once lead the nation in creating new corporations, but when business operating expenses get too high, corporations outsource projects to a state where income taxes are lower.

A healthy business climate creates and keeps jobs. Until recently, California citizens never thought businesses would leave the state. Former Governor Davis (and current Governor Brown) supported organized labor legislation, raising the cost of wages. One example being that overtime must be paid after eight hours per day, versus most other states that define overtime as anything over forty hours a week. This costs California businesses an extra $1 billion a year and slows job growth.

Is California Cap-and-Trade in Trouble?

Cap-and-Trade *is a government-mandated, market-based approach to controlling pollution by providing economic incentives for achieving reductions in the emissions of pollutants.* **It is mandatory.**

California's carbon dioxide cap-and-trade auction program, expected to bring in more than $2 billion in the current fiscal year.

Five hundred million of this expected sum is earmarked for Governor Brown's **High-Speed Rail Project** that was narrowly approved by voters in a ballot initiative. Because of uncertainty of its success, a $500 million reserve was built into the cap-and-trade budget. The August 2016 auction fell 98.5 percent short, so the entire $500 million reserve was consumed in the first of four auctions for the fiscal year.

As a further complication, a lawsuit is pending against the legality of California's cap-and-trade program. Business groups and fiscal conservatives claim the program amounts to a tax that would require a two-thirds majority vote of the legislature.

At the same time, the High-Speed Rail Project, which was promised to cost "only" $68 billion to run from the Bay Area to Los Angeles, will be facing $50 billion in overruns. To fund the rail system, which was sold to voters as not costing a dime in new taxes, the expected revenue stream from cap-and-trade has been "securitized." **This puts the state on the hook to Wall Street for billions in construction money advanced on the promise of future nonexistent cap-and-trade revenue.**

California should expect continued job growth and reduced unemployment figures over the next three years, according to the UCLA Anderson Forecast released in 2017.

The increase in U.S. job growth rates from construction, automobile sales, and business investment, as well as higher consumer demand, will continue to fuel our local economy.

Economists have a positive outlook for housing, since requests for permits for new construction have been increasing.

Consumer spending and residential house and condo sales are expected to drive economic and job growth from 2017 to 2020.

A. IS CALIFORNIA UNFRIENDLY TO BUSINESS?

California is not friendly to commerce.

Lured by many states' lower taxes, reduced costs, and less regulation, businesses are packing up to leave to growing states like Texas and Utah.

Despite being named by *Chief Executive* magazine as the worst state in the nation to do business for a decade, California will remain strong due mainly to our superior tech industries.

Riding the latest high-tech boom and an overall statewide surge, California recently leapfrogged France to become the world's sixth-largest economy.

Even with a reputation for being unfriendly to businesses, the state remains an economic powerhouse due in large part to the quality of talent in the digital and biotech industries.

Experts say employee skills, from a workforce composed of students from community colleges, state colleges, and universities, coupled with a vast amount of private equity, great weather, a range of attractions, and its geographic connection to investment from the rest of the Pacific Rim and Asia, will continue to keep California's economy growing.

B. COMPANIES (AND RESIDENTS) ARE FLEEING CALIFORNIA'S BURDENSOME TAX ENVIRONMENT

California's "skyrocketing" housing costs and high (corporate and personal) tax rates have prompted an "exodus of corporations and residents."

During the 12 months ending June 30, the number of people leaving California exceeded the number who moved here from elsewhere in the U.S., by 61,100, according to state Finance Department statistics. People are tired of the expense of living here. They are fed up with the endless taxes and getting nickel-and-dimed by the state of California every time they turn around.

Many large corporations have left the state recently, taking jobs (and employees) with them.

For example, in 2016, the parent company of Carl's Jr., founded in Anaheim, California, over 60 years ago, relocated its headquarters to Nashville, Tennessee, where there is no state income tax.

Even more recently, Nestlé USA, the maker of Häagen-Dazs, Baby Ruth, Lean Cuisine, and dozens of other mass brands, will have moved its U.S. headquarters from California to Virginia by 2018.

Northrop Grumman Corporation moved its headquarters out of California, leaving our state that gave birth to the aerospace industry without a single major military contractor based here.

In addition to high corporate taxes, many California cities (including Los Angeles and San Francisco) have adopted ordinances that are perceived as "meddling" in private sector hiring policies. One example is the "ban-the-box" ordinance that eliminates the checkbox on job applications that reveal criminal history of applicants.

If it did not have so much burdensome regulation and taxes, California would be growing much faster than Texas, given California's immense advantages (such as our pleasant climate and strong economic engines like Silicon Valley). But as it is, some multi-state businesses have closed their facilities in California, despite having plenty of customers, after experiencing pointless harassment due to California's oppressive regulatory regime, or the threat of meritless lawsuits.

C. CALIFORNIA BUDGET DEFICIT RISING: WASTEFUL SPENDING AND MINIMUM WAGE HIKES ARE TO BLAME

California's projected budget deficit is rising. Governor Jerry Brown's administration miscalculated costs for the state Medi-Cal program by $1.9 billion last year, an oversight that contributed to Brown's projection of a deficit in the upcoming budget.

By 2023, the minimum wage will reach $15.00 an hour in California giving businesses one more reason to leave the state, and adding a burden to an already large budget deficit.

California also spends its transportation dollars very poorly, and it is wasting billions on a high-speed rail boondoggle that few people will ride. As *Reason* magazine notes, federal transportation officials are warning that California's misnamed "bullet train" is a disaster in the making: they believe California is drastically understating the costs of its massive high-speed rail project. Just the first leg of this $70 billion project could cost billions more than budgeted. The project is at least seven years behind schedule.

No one disagrees with President Trump's statements that the nation's infrastructure is crumbling. The question is how will we pay for the repairs of California's airports, highways, bridges, and ports without going deeper into our already insurmountable debt?

Will Automation Create the Largest Job Loss in History?

Advanced automation techniques are the basic result of artificial Intelligence. The application of artificial intelligence (AI) is the exciting and disruptive field of automation. However, advanced automation has certainly become the most controversial.

Advancements in technology have already appeared in several sectors of the U.S. economy, mostly in the form of automation in banking and manufacturing. But one can see plenty of other industries that may experience a risk to their human labor force because of the automation of job functions. Examples include online banking, driverless trucks, and fast-food self-serving kiosks. The U.S. Treasury warns us that online banking automation is here, as fewer people want to go into their bank.

The potential for simultaneous and rapid disruption, coupled with the breadth of human functions that AI might replicate, may have profound implications and adjustments for many labor markets. Economists should seriously consider the possibility that millions of people may be at risk of unemployment, as many of these technologies are widely adopted.

Automation-safe professions basically require lots of creativity, direct personal service, and emotional judgments.

Automation is just one form of AI that has set up the U.S. to lose one half the number of banking jobs in the next five years and over 80 million jobs in other fields.

VII. Chapter Summary

The California state budget crisis is directly related to our slowing population growth. Our budget is constantly on the verge of deficit crisis, business taxes are at an all time high, and so are rents and home prices. Our state's resources cannot keep up with the added demands. California's schools are not improving, highways are congested, and more people live in poverty, relying on county and state human services.

The **state general fund budget** is the state government's financial plan for spending and taxing that is proposed by the governor and passed by the legislature for each fiscal year. A **deficit** occurs when the current money collected from the people, in the form of taxes, is not enough to pay for the agreed-upon expenses. The budget for now is balanced, but with the many disagreements with President Trump, how will we fair when it comes to getting our share of federal funds?

The four main source of taxes in California are **state personal income taxes, sales and use taxes, corporation taxes**, and **insurance taxes**.

A **regressive tax** is a tax that is larger as a percentage of income for lower income people. A **progressive tax** is a tax that increases as a percentage of income as the wealth of the taxpayer increases. **Sin taxes** are the taxes paid for the purchase and consumption of alcoholic beverages and tobacco products.

The four largest expenditures in California are **K-12 education, health care and human services, higher education**, and **corrections and rehabilitation**.

Earmarked funds are those that have been committed and budgeted ahead of time to accomplish a certain purpose. An example of earmarked funds are gas taxes.

A **bond** is a debt, a loan in increments of $1,000, made to the state of California, which will be repaid by the state to the owner of the bond on a certain date, usually in 20 years. A **general obligation bond** is secured by everything the state owns. A **revenue bond** is backed up only by the revenue generated by that project or taxing district.

California should expect continued job growth and reduced unemployment figures over the next three years—although automation may impact certain jobs dramatically.

The buzz seems to be that **California is not friendly to commerce**. But that is not entirely true. However, lured by lower taxes, reduced costs, and less regulation elsewhere, businesses are still packing up to leave.

But that's only half the story. Many entrepreneurs still see the Golden State as a ticket to success. Despite being named by *Chief Executive* magazine as the worst state in the nation to do business in 2014, California remains strong, many experts say.

In an average year, of the 32,000 companies that move annually, whether within California, out of the state, or into the state, only 1,700 in a year moved out of the state.

VIII. Class Discussion Questions

1. What types of taxes generate the most income?

2. List the main expenditures of the state and calculate what percentage of the budget is available for new programs.

3. Is the state sales tax or the state income tax more regressive or progressive in nature?

4. Of what significance is the fact that the state's population is growing younger?

5. When voters approve bonds, who will pay them off?

Index

This is a current list of topics that you as a well-informed student should grasp. You may even impress your friends with your political insights!

Chapter 1
"Trump Anxiety" boxes present both sides of emotional issues.

Chapter 2
President Trump is using federal powers to threaten California.

Chapter 3
Same-day voter registration and voting in 2018

Chapter 4
Legislative Transparency - 72-hour Internet notice required last minute changes in new laws.

Chapter 5
Increased cigarette tax to $2.87 a pack marijuana tax passed.

Chapter 5
Teacher and public employee pension debts threatens financial stability of California.

Chapter 6
Will state political leaders be battling President Trump's policies throughout his tenure?

Chapter 7
Our supermajority lawmakers passed a gas tax without need for voter approval.

Chapter 8
Will courts permanently block President Trump's funding threats against sanctuary cities and counties?

Chapter 9
Counties are financially okay, but our cities are in trouble

Chapter 10
Californian's taxing and spending is reckless and lopsided!

Dedicated to voters who love California and Politics. Why not join us? - **Walt Huber**